Hear the Children Crying

Hear the Children Crying

DALE EVANS ROGERS

With Frank S. Mead

Fleming H. Revell Company
Old Tappan, New Jersey

Scripture quotations in this volume are from the King James Version of the Bible.

Excerpt from THE FREEDOM OF FORGIVENESS by David Augsburger. Copyright 1970. Moody Press, Moody Bible Institute of Chicago. Used by permission.

Reprinted with permission of Macmillan Publishing Co., Inc. Excerpts from SOMEWHERE A CHILD IS CRYING by Vincent J. Fontana, M.D. Copyright © 1973 by Vincent J. Fontana.

Library of Congress Cataloging in Publication Data

Rogers, Dale Evans.
    Hear the children crying.

       1. Child abuse—United States. 2. Children's rights—United States. 3. Parent and child.
I. Mead, Frank Spencer, date   joint author.
II. Title.
HV741.R63   362.7'1   78-6703
ISBN 0-8007-0925-X

Contents

TO MY DAUGHTER

Dear Cheryl:

You were really the key to this book. It was through you, shortly after Debbie's death in 1964, that I became aware and a part of International Orphans, Incorporated. I was overjoyed as I watched your dedicated service in this fine organization formed by Yvonne Fedderson and Sara O'Meara, whose hearts and lives were profoundly touched and moved to help needy orphans of war and other parentless children who were too helpless to help themselves.

And it was through you and others in I.O.I. that I was honored with the first Woman of the World Award in recognition of my love and dedication to the welfare of children. Many moons have passed since then for you and those wonderful girls, and through you, many unfortunate children have been housed, fed, taught, ministered to, and adopted into lovingly receptive families.

Now you wonderful ones are again proving your faith in your great motto FIND A NEED AND FILL IT! in the organization of Children's Village, USA, where hapless, abused children and their parents can be treated together and rehabilitated mentally, physically, and spiritually.

This book is not written in any spirit of condemnation, but in concern over a terrifying, growing problem in our American society. Prayerfully, I have endeavored to go to the root cause of child abuse, which I believe—with all my heart—lies in the realm of spiritual poverty.

Thank you, girls of I.O.I., for your tireless efforts in behalf of "The heritage of the Lord"—our children. May God bless and increase your beautiful ministry of love.

Your loving and grateful mother,

Mom

DALE EVANS ROGERS

Do ye hear the children weeping, O my brothers,
  Ere the sorrow comes with years . . .
They are weeping in the playtime of the others,
  In the country of the free.
                    ELIZABETH BARRETT BROWNING
              from "The Cry of the Children"

Hear the Children Crying

1

Worse Than Watergate

The writers of books, usually, do their job for one of three reasons: fun, fame or fortune, and sometimes for all three reasons. That isn't why I wrote this book.

I wrote it not because I wanted to, but because I *had* to write it. There was no fun in it, and at my age, I am not particularly interested in fame or fortune. And there was another reason.

As a mother, I had always wanted and finally had a large-size brood of children, and I accepted the biblical dictum that to spare the rod on any of these children would be to spoil them. That seemed sensible and proper, whenever they got out of line. It came under the heading of correction, and they *needed* correction, when it got to be just too much. But I also knew that there was a time to drop the rod, lest I overdo it. Roy and I tried never to overdo it, never let correction become abuse. Still, there were times when I would lose my temper before flashing a prayer and counting ten before going to work on that section of the youngster's anatomy that was meant to be spanked. And when it was over, I asked their forgiveness for going too far in this necessary discipline. I reminded them: "I love you," and they knew that I meant it.

But this was not child "abuse." Hopefully, that word could never be applied to *me*. I thought of abuse as the work of a demented or alcoholic or drugged mother or father. I would mutter to myself that such people ought to be locked up for at least twenty years—and forgot it.

15

Then I was shocked into understanding that child abuse
and neglect is not a matter of some few local incidents but
a national epidemic in our country, and that it is high
time we got together and did something about it.

It is a sin and a crime and it has been rightly described
as a "disgrace worse than Watergate"—and I can no
longer "hold my peace" and ignore it.

2

The Problem

It all started, I think, one day when I was down in Tennessee recording an album. In my hotel room I picked up a newspaper and read an article that brought tears to my eyes and horrified me into stunned silence. It was a report on several cases of child abuse; it told of a father (*father!*) who stabbed his four-year-old son and then cut out one of the boy's eyes; another, of a woman and her common-law "husband" killing her two-year-old baby girl by forcing her into a tub of scalding water; and still another of a stepmother in California who chained a small child to a bedpost and beat her almost into insensibility—for wetting her bed!

This last woman, believe it or not, is quite typical of those in the abusive fraternity. She was of middle-class background, well groomed and seemingly quite intelligent. Neighbors called the police and told them that screams were coming *regularly* from that house. When the police arrived they found two small boys cowering behind the living-room sofa, frightened and afraid to answer any questions. (That silence is typical too.)

Another story told of a man who forced a four-year-old to walk until her feet were bleeding, and made her drink a hot sauce when she begged for water. A nine-year-old boy was banged against a wall until his skull was crushed beyond repair; he was dead on arrival at the hospital. Said the would-be mother, "He drove me nuts. He cried all the time."

I was suddenly so sick that I had to lie down. Then I was mad—so raging mad that I wanted to see the same ghastly punishment inflicted on *all* perpetrators of child abuse.

For many a long night, I could hear those children crying.

Not the Answer

Then I simmered down, and reminded myself of the words of Ephesians 4:26: "Be ye angry and sin *not* . . . ." (italics mine). There is indeed such a thing as righteous anger, but there is also a time when the anger should stop. Anger isn't the answer to this problem. It doesn't do any good or solve the problem just getting mad about it and then taking out our anger on such parents. Throwing such people into prison doesn't cure it! All too often, prison serves only to make the criminal a more educated convict. We can't just sweep it under the rug with a long prison sentence and forget it.

The words of Jesus flashed in my mind: "Take heed that ye despise not one of these little ones . . ." (Matthew 18:10), and "Suffer the little children to come unto me, and forbid them not: for of such is the kingdom of God" (Mark 10:14).

Right there is the ultimate wickedness of child abuse: it is well-nigh impossible for any child to come unto Jesus Christ and to love God and man, under such treatment. To me, one of the saddest sights in this world is that of a child robbed of his potential of faith in a God who loves him. I have come to believe with all my heart that we must fight such robbery of childhood with all that is within us.

An Ancient Sin

It isn't anything new. It is an old, old sin. Primitive people had a custom which called for the killing of one's third and fourth newborn children. In Old Testament times (Leviticus 18:21), the pagans sacrificed little children (babies) in the fiery furnaces of a deity called Molech. Later, in the time of Jesus, mothers in Rome, in perfect ease of mind and conscience, came out at night to leave unwanted babies at the foot of the infamous Lactarian column, there to die or be picked up by witches, slave dealers, or degenerates who would train them to be prostitutes or maim or cripple them and put them out on the streets to beg. The great Roman, Quintilian, rages against it: "To kill a man is often held to be a crime, but to kill one's own child is . . . a beautiful custom!" But Seneca, Plato, and Aristotle approved of the killing of defective children.

Infanticide was common as late as the Middle Ages. So was "swaddling"—the wrapping of babies so tightly that they could not move their arms or legs; often they were subject to gangrene—but, after all, it was easier to "control" them that way! Parents would take their children to see the bodies of hanged criminals swinging in the wind, and often whipped their children afterwards, so they would never forget that crime didn't pay.

In a *Psychology Today* article "Our Forebears Made Childhood a Nightmare," we read that one nineteenth-century schoolmaster who kept score of his punishments admitted administering 911,527 strokes with a stick, 124,000 lashes with a whip, 137,715 slaps with his hand and 1,115,800 boxes on the ear. William Buchan, a British pediatrician, said, "Almost half of the human species

perish in infancy by improper management and neglect."
A clergyman in England said that his parish was filled
with "suckling infants," and that in the space of one year,
he buried all but two of them. John Milton's wife complained that she had to listen to the cries of his nephews
as he beat them. Even royal little Louis XIII of France was
whipped for the sins of the previous day, when he got out
of bed in the morning. And William Penn once said that
"men are more careful of the breed of their horses than
they are of their children."

The children have had a tough time of it all down
through history. But—of course—all this was "way back
there" in the early ages, before we became civilized.
We're not like that *now*.

The "Civilized" Seventies

Oh, no? If you believe that (and many Americans do
believe it), then I refer you to a statement made by Dr.
Vincent J. Fontana, who is Medical Director of New York
City's Foundling Hospital. With such a background, he
should know what is going on *now*. He writes in *Somewhere a Child Is Crying:*

> Parents bash, lash, beat, flay, stomp, suffocate,
> strangle, gut-punch, choke with rags, or hot
> pepper, poison, crack heads, open, slice, rip,
> steam, fry, boil, dismember. They use fists, belt
> buckles, straps, hairbrushes, lamp cords, sticks,
> baseball bats, rulers, shoes and boots, lead or
> iron pipes, bottles, brick walls, bicycle chains,
> pokers, knives, scissors, chemicals, lighted ciga-
> rettes, boiling water, steaming radiators and
> open gas flames.

Brutal, isn't it? Yes—and a brutality that is far from decreasing. Doctor Fontana calls child abuse the Number One killer of American children, ". . . probably the most common cause of death in children today, outnumbering those caused by any of the infectious diseases, leukemia or automobile accidents." He declares it is a myth that in this nation we love our children.

It is next to impossible to keep as accurate a record as was kept by the old British schoolmaster, for the reason that there are undoubtedly many more *unreported* cases that never reach the ears of the police or the court judges. The figures we have do not tell the whole story: they are only the tip of the iceberg. But we do have figures and statistics that are interesting, to say the least.

Every two minutes, in the United States, a child is being attacked by one or the other of its parents . . . The American Humane Association reports the abuse of 307,000 children in just one year—1975 . . . the annual incidence of sexual abuse is put at from fifty to seventy-five thousand . . . New York City alone has thirty thousand *reported* abuse cases a year . . . one hundred thousand youngsters in the country are emotionally neglected . . . another one hundred thousand are physically, morally, and educationally neglected . . . . at least seven hundred are killed by their parents or parent surrogates . . . .

If the rate continues to rise as it is rising now, we can expect to find ourselves faced with a figure of a million and a half children either seriously maimed or crippled or killed *annually*.

Read it and weep!

Child Pornography

We get "all hot and bothered" over those ancient Roman mothers who abandoned their children to witches or slave dealers or the merchants of porn—but before we condemn them too much we might take a look at child porn as it is practiced in the United States in modern times. It is a billion-dollar business. Much of it is photographic business, a traffic in film and still photographs of children in sex acts or posing in the nude. *Time* magazine (April 4, 1977) quoted the Cook County (Illinois) Attorney General Bernard Carey as saying that pornographic pictures of children as young as five and six were available in Chicago; it also told the story of an Episcopal priest who ran a farm for wayward teenagers in Tennessee, who was awaiting trial on charges that he staged orgies with boys on the farm and mailed the pictures to so-called donors around the country.

Into our major cities pours a steady stream of runaway children between the ages of ten and seventeen; a survey conducted by the Department of Health, Education and Welfare reveals that 733,000 youngsters between those ages stay away at least overnight, and that "they are running away from emotional, physical and sexual abuse." If they make for the big city, they stand a good chance of meeting a disgusting "welcoming committee" the minute they get off the bus or the train—a "committee" of photographers ready and willing to pay them five or ten dollars or only the price of a meal for posing in a sex picture. Frightened and bewildered, they are quite likely to accept it. Lloyd Martin, the head of the sexually abused child unit of the Los Angeles Police Department, says, "Some-

times, for the price of an ice-cream cone, a kid of eight
will pose for a [film] producer. He usually trusts the guy
because he's getting from him what he can't get from his
parents—love."

I will surely be accused of exaggerating about child
porn, but a good look at just one city—New York—will
prove that I am not. We see it at its worst in Manhattan:
police surveys tell us that there are no less than twenty
thousand runaway girls on the streets—aged sixteen or
under. They come from all over the country—from small
towns and large in the Midwest and the West. (Eighth
Avenue in New York City has been nicknamed the "Minnesota Strip"; Minneapolis cops admit that some four
hundred juvenile girls from their town have been found
living as prostitutes in other cities, and that most of them
end up in New York City.) It is suspected that mobsters of
the Syndicate have moved into the racket and are slowly
taking over.

There are other parents who manage to keep the child at
home and still profit in the porn market. A social worker
in Illinois was recently sent to jail for allowing his three
foster sons to pose in a sex film for one hundred fifty
dollars each. Another pair of parents in Colorado was accused of selling their twelve-year-old son to a Texas man
for three thousand dollars.

At Last—A New Federal Law

I read with real joy in this morning's paper that President Carter has signed into law a bill forbidding the use of
children under sixteen in the production of pornographic

material. It prohibits the interstate transportation of any child for the purpose of prostitution or other commercial exploitation, and bans the sale and distribution of obscene material that depicts any child in sexually explicit conduct. The measure provides penalties of up to ten years in prison with a ten-thousand-dollar fine for first offenders, and up to fifteen years in prison with a fifteen-thousand-dollar fine for second offenders. The new law is called The Protection of Children Against Exploitation Act of 1977. It is my understanding that the idea is to define child pornography as a form of abuse rather than a form of obscenity. When "obscenity" is referred to, many so-called freethinkers insist that it is a violation of the First Amendment.

As happy as I am to see this new bill finally a signed law, may I add a word of caution. I have a feeling that it will take more than a law to wipe this thing out of existence. It will take a lot of plain citizen help, if you know what I mean. Those of us who remember Prohibition will remember that there were simply not enough of our people who believed in that law enough to make it work. It takes a lot of good citizen morality to make a good law effective.

Times Square Yesterday and Today

Now I know there will be some readers who will think I make too much with all this, or that I am too "selective" in my materials. Okay, reader—but before you say that, come and take a walk with me in New York's Times Square.

Times Square! Long, long ago, when I was fighting my way up in show business, I saw a movie musical called

Forty-second Street starring Dick Powell and Ruby Keeler. That movie put stars in my eyes, for Broadway and Forty-second Street (Times Square) in those days was symbolic of the dazzling top, with its marquees twinkling the names of famous entertainers who had "made it big." The sidewalks of Times Square were crowded with people on their way to really fine and decent entertainment. There was no fear of a mugging in Times Square in those days, and you weren't accosted by prostitutes; and there were no cheap "peep shows" to snare kids and adults alike, nor any darkened entrances to theaters specializing in smut.

That was *yesterday*. Today it is a different Times Square. Roy and I walked it recently, and we were sickened and infuriated at what we saw. The spectacle of women walking the sidewalks as prostitutes soliciting business was bad enough, but there was something worse than this. The *young* girls! They looked *so* young. They walked aimlessly, hopelessly, glassy-eyed—often in what seemed to be abject fear. It was horrible.

We walked past windows displaying invitations to buy books and pamphlets and pictures that would offend a self-respecting garbage can; the store owners called it "literature"; I call it *poison*. We were invited to "come in and enjoy live sex, performed right before your eyes." Some theatre marquees advertised pictures filthy beyond description. I knew, as I looked at it, what General William Booth of the Salvation Army meant when, as a young man walking through a particularly bad section of London's East End, he said, "I felt as though I were walking on the bottom floor of hell."

I watched a recent TV program based on a survey of the

porn problem in New York City; it demonstrated very clearly that the many young girls came to this district as runaways and remained as prostitutes. Once those girls were caught in the trap, they found themselves with no other place to go.

I sit comfortably in my California home and read the story of one young girl who got out of the Times Square trap. She was fifteen years old; she was found dead on a rooftop just off Forty-second Street. How she died we shall probably never know; we do know that she died without a single person near her to offer any help, to care whether she lived or died. She ended up on the rubble heap when she was no longer of any use to those who would exploit her.

Times Square! There is something like it, I suppose, in many large cities all over the world. A film director was arrested recently on charges that he had drugged and molested a thirteen-year-old girl he had hired for photographing. The pictures he got, I understand, were circulated in magazines published in *foreign* countries. This is an international traffic.

William Booth did something about what he found on hell's lowest floor: he founded the Salvation Army. There are a few like him working in Times Square, but they are pitifully few. The rest of us joke about it, or just pass by on the other side, like the priest and the Levite in Jesus' story of the Good Samaritan.

Battered Parents

I ran on a strange thing in doing research for this book: I learned that *very* often, battered children have parents who were abused when *they* were children. Doctor Fontana (quoted above) said in an interview:

> If you go into the background of battering parents, you are likely to find that they were abandoned in one way or another and did not feel love, affection, and security. They may have been shuttled from one foster home to another; or they may have been abandoned by one or both of their parents. They may be children of separation and divorce, or children from alcoholic family situations. They never "belonged" emotionally. They were deprived of loving, secure family situations. Consequently, as adults they are unable to give love, because in order to give love they must have had the experience of being loved.
>
> Interview by Edward Wakin,
> *U.S. Catholic*, March, 1974

His argument is backed by a survey made under the direction of Dr. Shervert Frazier, who studied the records of ninety adult murderers in Texas and Minnesota. All ninety, he says, ". . . were found in their childhoods to have been victims of brutality—beaten by alcoholic parents, choked, shoved outside naked in the snow, thrown against glass doors. It is hardly to be wondered at that, as adults, they should have treated others in the same violent way in which they had been treated as children. What is surprising is that the connection between child abuse and adult crime has not been stressed more vigorously" (from *America*, May 28, 1977).

Now let's look at three murderers we all know about:

Lee Harvey Oswald, who killed President Kennedy; Jack Ruby, who shot Lee Harvey Oswald; and Charles Manson, who went into the business of murder on a wholesale plan.

Lee Harvey Oswald, born in New Orleans, October 8, 1939 . . . Father died two months after Lee was born . . . Mother practically ignored him for his first six years . . . placed in an orphanage at three when his mother went out to work . . . at four was moved to Dallas, Texas, where mother married her third husband . . . Mother separated from her third husband in 1946 . . . Lee started school at Benbrook, Texas . . . moved to Covington, Louisiana . . . Lee in first grade in school . . . moved to Fort Worth, Texas . . . Mother finally divorced her third husband . . . Lee's record for five and a half years in Fort Worth was average but got steadily worse every year . . . moved to New York City at twelve . . . left alone often by his mother.

Lee developed emotional and psychiatric problems of potentially serious nature . . . sent to Youth House (a detention home) in New York City for truancy . . . a social worker said that he was "seriously detached" and "withdrawn," but that there was "a rather appealing quality about this starved, affectionless youngster" . . . he told a social worker that his mother did not care for him and regarded him as a burden . . . he had fantasies about being powerful and hurting people . . . chief psychiatrist at Youth House said the boy had "a personality pattern disturbance and schizoid features and passive-aggressive tendencies."

Lee was emotionally disturbed and needed psychiatric

treatment, which he did not get . . . returned to public school, where every one of his teachers complained of him as quite a disturbed youngster . . . Lee now on probation . . . Mother insisted she needed no help . . . Mother took him to New Orleans, where neighbors remembered him as a solitary but quite articulate boy . . . at sixteen he dropped out of school and tried to enlist in the U.S. Marine Corps—rejected . . . worked at several different jobs and started to read Communist literature . . . moved back to Fort Worth in 1956, entered high school . . . lasted two weeks . . . dropped out and got into the Marine Corps six days after his seventeenth birthday . . . comrades in the marines thought he was a sulky loner who resented authority.

So this was the childhood of Lee Harvey Oswald: neglected by a mother who gave him no love or affection; moved around from one so-called home to another, one city after another, never feeling safe or secure; left to himself, described as "dangerous, explosive, aggressive, and assaultive" at thirteen; the bewildered son of a mother who refused to cooperate with anyone who wanted to help—social workers, psychiatrists, court officers, probation officers—who said that she would do as she pleased and this was her own business! *This* produced a boy withdrawn into a fantasy world of his own, who was forced to distrust everybody and was fearful of any authority. All through these formative years, Oswald slowly developed "a towering rage" against women, and all of his life he resented the fact that he was fatherless. Danger was building up in him all that time—and nobody found a way to really help him, or change, or save him—right up to the day when he got a president in the sights of his rifle and pulled the trigger. It all surfaced, all exploded in this final, hideous act—*and it need never have been so!*

Jack Ruby? Ruby was born in Chicago, April 19, 1911 . . . the third of eight children of an alcoholic father who deserted his family . . . his mother was in and out of several mental hospitals . . . put in a foster home for two years . . . had only one year of high school . . . a street hustler in his teens . . . the victim of psychomotor epilepsy . . . an underprivileged boy with only one way to go . . . .

Charles Manson? Manson was born (an illegitimate) in Cincinnati, Ohio, November 11, 1934 . . . never saw his father . . . sent by his prostitute, alcoholic mother to live with a grandmother and an aunt who punished him severely . . . at fourteen he rented a room of his own . . . ran messages for Western Union . . . became a petty thief . . . said he was ashamed of his mother, who was living in sin.

Charles was turned over successively to several schools for wayward boys as well as to the famed Boys Town in Nebraska (where a priest said he was badly in need of attention and affection), to a reformatory for stealing a motor scooter and a car, and to the National Training School for Boys in Washington, D.C. . . . spent his first thirteen years with a drinking prostitute for a mother and the next twelve years in various reformatories or prisons.

After all that, he and his "family" staged an orgy of murder in which five people were slaughtered. This "family" talked much of love, and what a grim, obnoxious love it was. They seemed to know everything about sex and nothing about real love, but it is still startling and shocking to hear Charles Manson say, "That's all there is, man. If you don't have someone to love you, you don't have anything." (Think about *that!*)

If Only . . . .

Some years back there appeared an interview in *Christian Herald* with the famous Warden Lewis Lawes of Sing Sing Prison. At the time, a young man named Crowley was in the death house, awaiting execution for murder. The warden described Crowley: a boy born of a drunken father and mother, forced out into the street before he was even old enough for school, forced to steal in order to eat. He stole little brass bars from a nearby railroad yard, at first, then robbed small stores; then murdered during a robbery.

Said the warden, "That boy never had a chance to be anything but what he is right now, or of winding up anywhere but behind the bars."

He opened his desk drawer and pulled out a sheaf of pen-and-ink drawings as beautifully done as any professional artist might do them—drawings of flowers, mountains, beautiful girls—and, said the warden, "Young Crowley did *this*. He *could* have been a great artist, if only . . . ."

If only *what?*

In *A Child Is Being Beaten,* Naomi Feigelson Chase writes, "The less care a child has in the early years, the more society will pay for it later on."

That's *what.*

We could go on and on with this; we could offer a

thousand illustrations of the fact that child abuse tends to produce more child abuse, from one generation to another. Any good sociologist or social worker or policeman will tell you that. But let me sum it up with this little piece which I have just read in *Frontiers,* published by Parents Anonymous. It is entitled "Thoughts From Inside":

December 27th is the day—
The day I love and fear,
For on this day, I remember
The spiritual joy of my daughter's birth—
Bright moments when we were near
And the body-shattering agony of her death.

I think of her alive and vital—
An extension of myself, really . . . a tiny twin.
We spoke without words, loved without doubt,
Truly we were two children as one,
Her beauty moves me still:
Her voice . . . as sweet as an angel's song.

Wise she was . . . in her eyes I saw it—
The wisdom of those eyes tortured me.
Mother? Drunk, whore, broke, scared,
A poor mother was I, in every way but love,
But my pitiable efforts to survive kept me rigid.
It would have been better to scream for help.

Too many motels, too much booze, too little warmth,
Too many nights with a car as our only home.
Too many hungry times, and times beaten and raped.

I told myself it was all for her—
She was with me . . . and she saw it all,
I thought she understood the ugliness,
And her eyes were wise.

With such a beginning, how could she be?
Would she be defeated and without . . . like me?
I loved her so . . . my soul cried, "No!"
And when she died, there was relief in grief—
It seems that she had escaped and was with Light now.
My love, warm as ever, wished her peace and pride.

Contributions from the Members
Inside California Institution for Women
at Frontera

I don't know how this will strike you, but it shook me up. I would not fit into the mother pattern of this piece of verse, and neither would you—but it still makes us wonder about the whole bitter problem of child abuse—wonder who is really responsible for it all.

Let's have a look at that in the next chapter.

3

The Parents

By this time you may begin to see that what we have here isn't a child problem, but a parent problem. Child abuse is an *adult* disease. We get there too late with too little, when we treat only the abused *child*.

Behind the beaten child is a disturbed parent, often a parent trying to cope with other contributory problems over which he or she has lost control. One Denver mother who feared she would some day choke her child to death expressed her feelings with this:

> Although I love him very much, my nervousness leads me to do things I often disapprove of at the time, and if I don't disapprove of my actions at this time, I frequently disapprove of them later . . . . Many times. After I beat him he would lie in his crib and cry himself to sleep. I would sit next to the crib and cry and wish I could beat myself.
>
> From *The Battered Child,*
> by Ray E. Helfer and C. Henry Kemper

The Parent As Victim

Doctor Kemper says something here that may make you stop and look and listen: "I regard them [parents] as victims; I have a very hard time not feeling sorry for them."

You have to know what and who the abusive parents are in order to understand that statement. Contrary to what many of us think, they are *not* an easily identified tribe of born savages. Less than 10 percent of them are psychotic or mentally ill, but the other 90 percent are *emotionally* ill. They are upper class, middle class, lower class, rich, poor, educated, uneducated, laborers, executives, farmers, clerks, blue collar and white collar, religious, agnostic, and atheist. They live in large cities, in suburban towns, in slums and mansions. The average age of mothers: twenty-six; of fathers: thirty. You could look at almost any one of them and say, "Oh, not that one; he couldn't possibly be a child abuser," and you could be wrong.

You will find a few who seem to be monsters; an estimated 5 to 10 percent are sadists, but that's only a small part of the picture. Most of them are quite ordinary people who cannot cope with stresses and distresses forced upon them. Often they are socially isolated, and many of them have wracking marital and financial problems that beat upon them and wear them down. A high percentage of them are alcoholics; a small percentage are on drugs. The incidence of abuse is highest in families that are poor, thanks to low income and unemployment and bad housing and depressive general poverty. Add to that the too-many young unmarried girls having babies and the ease with which divorce is possible (40 percent of American marriages end up in divorce court) and you have a general idea of what causes the trouble.

One black mother nailed it down when she said, "It isn't the kids that need help. The problem is, how do you help the parents?"

Generally speaking, there are four types of child abuse: physical, verbal, emotional, and sexual. May I suggest another that I think important: conscious or unconscious *neglect?*

Neglect

Neglect is a form of abuse born out of a lack of love or out of plain (and often unconscious) carelessness. When a child comes to a father or mother with a question that is serious to him, hears the parent duck the question, or turn it off with "Don't bother me now, son; later, later . . ."—*that* parent is guilty of abuse through neglect. When the parents are too busy with their own affairs to correct or help, they are guilty of a carelessness that to me is just plain criminal.

Still, much of it is *unconscious* neglect.

Just this past weekend, Frances Williams (who is manager of the box office of our Museum in Victorville, California) told me of a touching incident of neglect with a happy ending. A man with seven(!) children came to see the museum and they were inside for quite a while. Francie was busy, and she did not see them leave the building. Some time later she saw a little boy wandering around the lobby with a look of lostness and bewilderment on his face. Always sensitive to the needs of children, she asked the youngster if she could help him. He said he couldn't find his father. Francie got one of the other girls to take over in the office, took the little fellow by the hand and went looking for the rest of the family. No luck. Apparently, this one had fallen behind the rest of the group, and the father had neglected to count noses when they left.

She told the boy not to worry; they would find his father; they would go over to the sheriff's office and report the lost child—and lost father! Then she would take him home with her, after closing time, and they'd have a good time until his father came back. The boy seemed a little doubtful about all this, and he went outside to look at Trigger, who stands out in front of the museum rearing up as though he were still alive. The boy kicked at the stones out there and walked around in the lobby with anxiety written all over his face, trying not to cry. Just as they were ready to lock up, a car came screeching around the corner of the building and the frantic father leaped out and gathered the child in his arms. They had driven possibly fifty miles before he realized that one of his tribe was missing! Now they roared off down the road, with everybody waving and laughing and cheering. All's well that ends well.

My mother told me of a similar experience, when she was on a train in the custody of my maternal grandmother. In the crush and rush to get off at their destination, her mother left one of her children sleeping on the train. Both the child and mother were terrified. Happily, they were united easily, but "Mama" counted noses after that!

Now none of us would condemn the unintentional neglect of either that man at the museum, or of my good old grandmother. But the children involved really suffered an unnecessary trauma, didn't they? There isn't much more to be said about unintentional neglect except, "Watch it, parent; even such neglect can have a disastrous effect on your child."

Sandy's Story

This still leaves us with intentional abuse and neglect, which tell a different story. I discovered what that meant with one of our own adopted children.

Little Sandy, our "adoptee," had the misfortune of being born to parents who beat him and starved him and left him to die in a motel room. We got him when he was only five years old, and at that early age (we soon found out), he was suffering from some brain damage, a deep hostility toward women (due to the mother's neglect of him), poor coordination, astigmatism in one eye, and a total inability to control his bladder (a *very* prominent excuse for child abuse).

His parents were both alcoholics; both had been in jail more than once. They had three other children whom they neglected when they were placed in foster homes. That's NEGLECT, in capitals! Sandy never had a birthday cake, or presents at any Christmas except for those cheap geegaws that he found in cereal boxes. He had curvature of the spine and rickets (never treated). He told us that he had to sleep in a big old armchair on an open porch. More than one morning he woke up to find his blanket covered with snow.

When we first brought him home, our pediatrician looked at us in amazement. He couldn't understand how we could adopt a child with such problems. Two years later the same pediatrician was amazed at the change in the child. We had given him love, and so . . . .

This change didn't come overnight, however. It came after a long struggle in which we often made mistakes and were driven almost out of our wits, especially by his bed-wetting. I confess that I was less than patient with him many, many times.

Our live-in help complained; his room stank, no matter how much disinfectant we used. I was determined to stop it, for the sake of Sandy's feelings of self-esteem as well as for my own feelings of irritation and helplessness. Often, after chastising him for his seeming apathy, I would go to my room, break into tears and ask for God's forgiveness—and patience—with *me*. I truly loved this boy and I wanted a future for him that was spiritually and physically and economically secure.

A Tough Assignment—Curing Enuresis

I can still remember those days and nights when our whole family derided Sandy and tried to shame him into conquering this childish curse of enuresis. When he had a dry night, everybody in the house rejoiced and made ready to kill the fatted calf for him, but when he had a bad night it was something else. We tried everything—even having him sleep on a rubber mat that was constructed to give him a slight electrical charge that set off a burglar-type alarm at the appearance of the first drop of moisture. This was combined with a police-interrogation light that hit him in the face. The first night it worked, and there was cheering. The second night everybody in the house woke up when the alarm went off, but Sandy snoozed peacefully through it all.

Then we gave him a plastic mattress, absorbent sheets, and warm blankets—and told him that he would have to hang them out on a line in the backyard to dry when he came home from school. I didn't realize what I was doing until I happened to see Mike Landon's TV broadcast, in which he, as a child, suffered the same cruel penalty. That was a perfect depiction of our problem. It made me realize how wrong I was, how guilty *I* was. I hadn't realized what that sort of "correction" could do to a child. I was guilty of child abuse and didn't know it!

A Letter to Cherish

We tried more gentleness, after that sad experiment, and it worked. He grew gradually into man's estate, as a normal, happy, dignified human being. In our Victorville Museum we have a letter from Sandy (then in the armored division of the United States Army), written several days before he died in Frankfurt, Germany. In this letter he thanked Roy and me for adopting him into a Christian home; he said that he hoped God would give him the faith and courage to establish the same kind of home for *his* children. He thanked us for our patience with him (how that burned my heart when I recalled those not-so-patient instances!). He never had a chance to do that, but we do thank God for sending this poor neglected child our way.

It *can* be done, even with the most unpromising of children. The trouble is that so many parents fail to realize their neglect of their child's right to grow in dignity and self-respect.

I love the words of François de la Fénelon: "If I were asked what single qualification was necessary for one who has the care of children, I should say *patience*—patience with their tempers, with their misunderstandings, with their progress."

The Norma Zimmer Story

Norma Zimmer, that gifted and beloved songstress for God, who stars on the "Lawrence Welk Show" and sings at the Billy Graham crusades, has a touching neglect story.

As Norma tells it, she was born into a poverty-stricken home and to a father and mother who just didn't want her. They already had two children; a third meant more of a burden than a blessing. The father drank heavily—taking out his frustration with a bottle and on his family. The mother drank, too—out of desperation. Norma was the "runt" of the family, and she was too often reminded of that.

Her father played the violin, and played it well, until the day he had his hand crushed in a shipyard accident. Denied fame and fortune and no longer able to play violin concerts, he demanded that his children become violinists—but they did not enjoy playing the violin. This made him furious. Norma's hands were too pudgy and too short for violin fingering—even too short for the piano. But she stayed with the violin and the piano through high school. Her high-school music teacher complimented her on her ability to read music, but she wasn't enjoying it. Her heart skipped a beat when the sympathetic teacher told her that she had a really good voice, and he encouraged her to cultivate that voice. But there was trouble even here. The teacher drilled her as a lyric soprano; the father insisted that she was a coloratura soprano and made her strain her vocal cords to reach F above High C. That meant serious damage to the throat, if she kept it up. It seemed that her father was interested only in throwing stumbling blocks in the path of every dream and ambition in her longing heart. Her only encouragement came from the schoolteacher, who got her into a church choir.

There may have been something wrong with her fingers, but there was nothing wrong with her voice. She was born to sing and she sang with a warm glow that spread out over the church congregation and seemed to touch the hearts of all of them. There were two in that congregation who needed warming that day: her father and her mother, who came to hear her sing her first solo. They came intoxicated and disheveled, stumbling over the feet of other people to reach seats in the middle of a row. The congregation stared . . . .

Norma was paralyzed with shame, as she got to her feet to sing: "How beautiful upon the mountains are the feet of him that bringeth good tidings . . . ." Then she sat down, repeating the words again and again, and something new—something she desperately needed—came over her. It climaxed when the minister in his sermon repeated the words of the first verse of the Forty-sixth Psalm: "God is our refuge and our strength, a tested help in time of trouble."

That was the greatest moment of her life. She says, "I realized how desperate life in our family was without God, and that day I committed my life to Him. Jesus came into my life not only as Savior but for daily strength and direction."

After that, the road was smoother—it was a different life. Norma Zimmer, with her talent devoted completely to God, was on her way to stardom.

What would she have been if this hadn't happened?

Emotional Explosions

". . . Child abuse," writes Claude A. Frazier in *Christianity Today*, "can be emotional, such as failing to provide love, attention, normal living experiences, proper supervision . . . . Emotional abuse can also include such things as constant belittling [Norma Zimmer!], scolding, nagging, yelling, and teasing. Abuse that is both emotional and physical abuse includes such assaults on a child's mind and body as incest and other indecent sexual activity within or outside the family."

Heaven have pity on any mother who suffers the buildup of emotion to the point when she can't take it any more. A woman up in Connecticut, where there is a Care Line telephone service to help parents with child-abuse problems, called one morning, almost screaming, "You gotta help me. I'm here alone and the baby is driving me crazy. He won't quit crying and I can't get out. His father's gone. Even the TV is busted. I've got to get away from this kid before I do something terrible. I feel like I want to kill him."

Unusual? It's unusual only in that the emotional maddened mother made a phone call; thousands of others with the same emotional problem don't phone—and then anything can happen, and usually does. This woman's desperation could be duplicated in thousands of homes. More than one perfectly good mother has been so worn down by her rambunctious children that she has been tempted to scream, "I'll kill him!" Of course she would never kill him; of course the emotional pot simmers down, almost instantly, and she is the loving mother once again.

The point is, however, that the emotions *can* pile up to the boiling point, and if the frantic mother or father has nowhere to turn for help, there can be a devastating explosion. Pile up the tensions of poverty, of a father out of work, of boredom, of frustration, of a mother who is virtually a prisoner with a child and totally unprepared for such a situation, and such a mother will feel imposed upon and will lash out at the child or children. Overwrought emotion is a fearful master.

The parents of another girl were convicted of keeping her in a tiny, dark cubicle for much of her eight years. The girl, when she was finally released, weighed only twenty pounds and had the bone structure of a child less than half her age. The parents had placed lighted cigarettes on her feet; she slept and ate in her two-by-five cubicle, never went out to play, never attended school. The woman's lawyer contended that she was a sick woman, and not responsible for her actions. Besides this, he said, she had been raped by the child's true father, and she explained her treatment of the girl with this:

"Every time I looked at her, I saw the face of that man who had raped me." But she showed little emotion when she was sentenced to a prison term on charges of child abuse, conspiracy, and false imprisonment. By that time, she had been drained emotionally dry.

Well, I have mixed emotions about such a case as this. I wonder why this mother didn't have her child adopted, or placed in a foster home, if she couldn't control her emotions. The rape was not the child's fault, but this mother, who was sick, sick, sick, paid the penalty for it in guilt, remorse, and emotional frenzy. I am not trying to excuse her for her crime, but only to find a logical explanation for why it happened. Given such circumstances, even a better mother might descend to the same depths.

The Lurking Tiger

Even the best of us have a tendency to "fly off the handle" emotionally. There is a lurking tiger under the skins of all of us—an emotional tiger who can be turned loose in an unguarded moment—to our lasting sorrow.

I read this little story in David Augsburger's book *The Freedom of Forgiveness:*

> There was once a tiger keeper and a tiger who lived together. The keeper wanted the tiger for a pet, a friend. He fed him, walked him, cared for him. He always spoke softly, warmly to him. But as the tiger grew, his green eyes began to glow with hostility. His muscles rippled their warning of power. One night, when the keeper was off guard, a lovely girl happened by. The claws reached out. There was a scream. The keeper arrived too late.
>
> Then others felt the tiger's teeth—a boy, a man. And the keeper in panic prayed that the tiger might die, but still he lived. In fear, the keeper caged him in a deep, dark hole where no one could get near. Now the tiger roared night and day. The keeper could not work or sleep through the roars of his guilt. Then he prayed that God might tame the tiger. God answered, "Let the tiger out of the cage. I will give you strength to face him." The keeper, willing to die, opened the door. The tiger came out. They stood. Stared. When the tiger saw no fear in the keeper's eyes, he lay down at his feet.
>
> Life with the tiger began. At night he would roar, but the keeper would look him straight in the eye, face to face again. The tiger was never completely in his power, although as the years

passed they became friends. The keeper could touch him. But he never took his eyes off him or off the God who had given him the strength to tame the beast. Only then he was free from the roar of remorse, the growl of guilt, the raging of his own evil.

Both keeper and tiger are you.

God has not offered to kill your tiger. Death will do that all too soon. But His offer is and has been the strength to tame that evil within. To master it, before it masters you. He can and will set you free from its tyranny.

Then He supplies the strength to live with your own passions, lusts, hostilities in check, so that the true you, made in God's own image, begins to live, and what a change. Christ called it a new birth. It's all that and more.

I wish that every abusive parent—or near-abusive parent—that every organization that counsels and comforts and treats these people who come to them for help—might read it and give it to their "patients." For when we come to the end of our own power to control our destructive emotions and ask God to take over, we are on our way to real help. We need Him desperately; we need to know what the psalmist means when he calls God a very present help in times of need. You can't beat that!

Discipline

The child abusers have an ancient and overworked excuse or explanation for their abuse: "He's my kid, isn't he? I have a perfect right to discipline him when he needs it." One mother drove a visiting social worker from her home with the words, "Get out of here and leave me alone. Stop butting in on something that is none of your business."

That idea grows out of an old tradition in our country—a tradition that the parents of American children, ever since Colonial days, have had a perfect right to discipline (spank) their children when they need it. Because the Puritans did it, *we* can and should do it. (Or, they quote the Bible: "Spare the rod and spoil the child.") That, they believe, is justification for the use of the rod.

They are fond of telling us that in the schoolroom, up to the last century, the schoolmaster "laid it on" his pupils with the approval of the parents. And as late as 1976, the Supreme Court gave its blessing to teachers in the public schools to paddle their pupils. That decision came out of the case of a fifteen-year-old girl who had been worked over with a paddle by three male school officials. There was quite a furor raised about it; it was suggested by other outraged parents that this was a punishment to be expected only in a prison—and it is even prohibited there!

I have mixed reactions to this. When I read of pupils in some of our city schools attacking their teachers, stabbing, and even attempting to rape them, I'm all for the use of the paddle. On the other hand, I hate to think of what some infuriated teacher might do to a child, if and when he lost his temper and laid it on abusively and dangerously. Children are not chattels; they have their rights, too, and those rights should be protected.

I read the story of one father who went all-out in his discipline. When the doctors in a hospital examined his child he saw trouble coming, and he tried to forestall it by saying, "When he is bad—and he is most of the time—I give him a gentle little tug on the ear . . . ." The doctors found that one of the boy's ears had been nearly severed from his head!

When Discipline Becomes Brutality

Being an old-fashioned "square," I can see certain advantages to be gained by the application of the parent's hand to "the seat of learning" of the young culprit. But I also believe that there is a firm line to be drawn between discipline and abuse. When rage swings the rod, when discipline gets out of hand and brutality takes over, the effect upon the child becomes something horrible. An official of the Massachusetts Society for the Prevention of Cruelty to Children cites examples of this in cases he had seen at his agency:

- A five-year-old girl went out on her porch when told to stay inside; she was disciplined by being kicked into the house, thrown against the wall, and struck on the head and face with a frying pan.
- A nine-month-old boy's eyes were blackened, his fingers, face, and neck burned, and his skull fractured by his father.
- A thirteen-month-old girl was X-rayed in a hospital; the pictures revealed multiple fractures and a state of subdural hematoma.
- X-rays on a seven-month-old boy revealed fractures of one arm, the other arm previously broken, healed fractures on both legs, and multiple skull fractures.

Discipline? Do we have the gall to call this *discipline?*
Are "parents' rights" as absolute as this? What of the
rights of the child? Dr. C. Henry Kempe, a noted authority in the field, denies this parental right of abuse: "A
child does not belong to its parents; he belongs to himself
in the care of his parents." So say I. To discipline a child
brutally is to create a deep hostility in that child, and it
can make *him* a child abuser in his turn, and it can turn
him into a thief or murderer, as it did with Oswald, Ruby,
and Manson.

Now I firmly believe that it is sometimes almost impossible for a parent to know where to draw the line between
punishment and abuse, unless that parent has a strong
religious faith. An abundance of love is needed between
parent and child. Discipline simply for discipline's sake,
without loving concern, is a violation of the child's rights
as an individual. The "spare-the-rod-and-spoil-the-
child" admonition of the Bible means to me that a *moder-
ate* application of the rod will be good for the child; it will
spare him a more fearful punishment applied by society
as he grows to manhood. But we must remember that,
being a child, he cannot help blundering and stumbling
as he learns the lessons of life (it would be good for the
parents to remember that they did a lot of blundering and
stumbling, when they were his age!).

The child needs to know what and whom he can trust
and depend upon. He needs to know the boundaries of
good and bad conduct and to know the consequences of
flagrant and continued disregard of those boundaries.
Otherwise, he becomes insecure. We parents need to be
consistent in rewards for good or bad behavior—but discipline must always be done with love. Even an animal is

safer, healthier, and happier with a loving master to train him.

Speaking of animals, it is odd but true that we Americans seem to be more concerned with preventing abuse to animals than we are in preventing cruelty to children. It is odd, too, that a church worker in New York City, seeking help for a battered child, had to turn to the American Society for the Prevention of Cruelty to Animals for help she could not find elsewhere. She got it, and it was the initial victory which led to the founding of the Society for the Prevention of Cruelty to Children! The animals came first.

A Lasting Memory

Now let me speak out of my own experience. I keep remembering my own childhood and the childhoods of my own now-grown-up children, as I write this. I knew beyond the faintest shadow of a doubt that my parents loved me; I knew that I also frequently misbehaved (a conservative statement!) and that I often merited a spanking. I also knew that they could be merciful in discipline, when they saw any sign of repentance on my part.

Once I was told to help my little brother throw some bricks over a fence in our backyard. I was furious; I wanted to play house with my dolls and my dishes. In my pout I threw the first brick too low; it hit the top of the fence and bounced back on my brother's head, cutting a deep gash in his forehead, perilously close to his eye. With tears spilling down my face and screaming in terror, I ran into the house shouting, "Mama, Daddy! I have killed my brother!" They came running, applied a bandage, and called the doctor while I stood sobbing.

I fully expected a whipping for that, but—no, I saw them feeling sorry for me, and that was punishment enough. I got a reprieve, but my brother carried that scar all his life and I think it has hurt me more than it ever hurt him. I did not *mean* to hurt him, and my parents knew it, so they let discipline take care of itself.

God understands the blundering and the stumblings of His children but He looks upon the *heart* of man, not on outward appearances. My Bible tells me that as a Father He "loveth and chasteneth" (*see* Revelation 3:19), but I have found that He more often blesses us because He loves us. He does not wish to destroy His children by abusive chastening; He only wants to create in them a good character that He can use.

My own children sometimes say to me, "Mom, when you really used to get on us, you often ruined it by saying, 'I'm sorry I lost my temper' afterwards because we really had it coming." These kids are often smarter than we think. We who are Christian parents seldom realize how closely we are watched by our children.

One of my sons-in-law, who was not a Christian when he married our daughter, told her, "Your mother's religion is a phony; it's just an act; you'll see." He watched me as a hawk watches a chicken—intently. But when the funerals of our Debbie and her little girl friend were over, and the Lord through His Holy Spirit had sustained and directed me and brought me through it, this same boy said to our daughter, "I was wrong about your mother's religion. She has something I need."

That something came to him: two months ago he was ordained a minister in the Free Will Baptist Church, with the approval and support and commitment of his wife and their two children who are equally committed to Jesus Christ. They are one in the Spirit in that family, and it is something beautiful to see. ". . . this is the Lord's doing, and it is marvelous in our eyes" (Matthew 21:42).

There will never be any child abuse in *that* house.

The Separated Ones

E. M. Forster, in his book *Where Angels Fear to Tread,* makes this statement about children and their parents: "All of a child's life depends on the ideal he has of his parents. Destroy that and everything goes—morals, behavior, everything."

Give a child parents he can love and it is nine to one that he will grow into a parent *his* children can love. Give him parents he cannot love, who quarrel around the clock, who think more of their own pleasure than they do of their children's; who get a divorce because they are too lazy or indifferent to face up to their marital problems; or who are not even married—give him this and you get an abused child who will grow up with a grudge against the world. Give him a mother so intent upon a career, so anxious to get her so-called rights that she denies all the rights of her child—and she gets what she deserves in children who despise her.

The divorce rate in this land of the free seems to be going up with every tick of the clock. Yesterday the statisticians said that four out of every ten marriages end up in divorce court; but that was yesterday. (I've read of some who don't even bother to get a divorce—inasmuch as they have never been married!) I do not know exactly what the divorce rate is at the moment, but I do know that it has become a national disgrace and that the separations involved are wreaking havoc on the children.

Gary

Take, for instance, the case of Gary Ellenberg, age eleven, who died not long ago in San Francisco. Gary's parents had been divorced, and he was shuttled back and forth between mother and father—endlessly. His father, just previous to the boy's death, had been searching for him for nearly five months and found him when it was too late—dead, in the intensive care unit of a hospital.

His thirty-four-year-old mother and her boyfriend, a former policeman, were arraigned on murder charges. She had taken Gary to the hospital, where she told the doctors that he would not eat and that he seemed to be deteriorating. Investigation proved that he had dropped to forty-four pounds, and that he had been handcuffed in the bathroom of the couple's apartment. That was to keep him from "running away." (Who wouldn't run away—from that?) Under legal custody following the divorce, the boy had lived first with the mother, then with the father, who had really tried to help him. He had encouraged him to join a Cub Scout pack and to play baseball in the Little League. Gary attended the Lakeshore School, where he was considered a good pupil and was well liked by his teachers and classmates. Apparently he was happy with his father, who was active in the Parent-Teacher organization in the school.

Gary spent some time with the mother, during these early years of the separation, and while she was strict with him, she was not found guilty of any of the charges brought against her. But the custody was changed so many times that the boy became confused and emotionally upset. Just when he had reached the point where he was getting along beautifully with the father, he was snatched away to live horribly with the mother and her boyfriend—and he just gave up. He couldn't take any more changes brought on by the divorce, and things went from bad to worse, and then came the handcuffs, and . . . .

Public indignation ran so high that serious consideration was given to a transfer of the trial of the mother and the boyfriend to another area, in the interests of a fair trial. But what difference did that make? Gary was dead.

Lost in the Battle

Of course, this does not happen to all children of divorce. They do not all die, but too high a percentage of them just drift into useless and meaningless living. The trauma of separation never quite leaves them. A little girl I love said to me, "I love Jesus better than anyone else in the world, better than my mommy and daddy." I am grateful for her faith, but I have trouble, sometimes, trying to be understanding toward the fighting between her divorced parents.

Yes, it is rough on the child of divorced parents—the child who finds himself torn between two battling parents who have somehow lost all love for each other. In the atmosphere of a home like that, the child is torn apart trying to understand, trying to keep from being lost in the battle:

Little girl lost, where is her place?
Wondering young eyes—sad little face,

How can she choose, one from the other?
On one side is Daddy—on another is Mother.
She should be happy; it seems such a shame
She has to suffer when she's not to blame.
She should be running, laughing, chasing
      butterflies,
Looking for a rainbow, catching fireflies.
Daddy and Mommy—feel all her fears!
Daddy and Mommy—see all her tears!
Stop fighting long enough to see
What your bitterness has cost—
Look at her! She's a little child lost!

                              DALE EVANS ROGERS

I believe that many divorces could be avoided and that many a pair of quarreling parents might be reconciled, if they honestly *wanted* it that way. But once they separate, once the divorce is finalized—well, that's it. The child suffers. Even then, I think, the parents might help, if they would guard against making derogatory remarks about each other in the child's presence. That can rob him of the last vestige of respect for either of them. He becomes evasive and untruthful, contradicting the values that he may have been taught when it was a happy home.

I am vulnerable on this question of the child victims of divorce, thanks to my own divorce experience. The father of my six-month-old son deserted us, asking for a divorce that I did not want, but which I was finally forced to accept. Thank heaven, my boy was too young to know what was happening at the time; he did not know the particulars of it all until he was past twenty years of age.

In his younger years, whenever the question came up, I would simply tell him that his father and I were too young, too emotionally immature to make our marriage work. I felt that as a child he had enough to worry about without inflicting on him my resentment of his father's desertion.

Remarriage didn't solve the problem, either, for I subconsciously carried my resentment into it. I was not yet a committed Christian, and I had a large economy-sized chip on my shoulder. In the effort to prevent myself or my son from being hurt again, I never really gave that second marriage the chance I would have given it if I had known the Lord of love and sacrifice in a personal way. Later, when I was once more contemplating divorce, I asked my boy how he felt about it, telling him that I was sorry to put him through the whole miserable performance again, and that I had always wanted the best for him—a good home, a good education, and a good future. He said quietly, "Mom, the best thing you could have done for me was to marry a man who really wanted me."

Fortunately, I had a mother—a truly Christian mother—who stepped in and gave the boy a good home and the influence of a good Gospel-believing church. Today I am more than proud of my son; I am truly grateful for him. He is a fine, totally committed Christian with three daughters who have been taught to seek first the Kingdom of God and His righteousness.

Women's Lib

I used to laugh at the thing called "Women's Lib," but I'm not laughing now. In its first days, it seemed logical

enough to me that women should stand in equality with
men; back then it appeared to be another phase of the
fight for women's liberation started on the political front,
by such women as Emmeline Pankhurst, Carrie Chapman
Catt, and Susan B. Anthony; but the *modern* lib movement
has grown into something quite different from that.
Today a really radical element is driving the lib horses. I
hear them shouting for some causes that are insignificant
to me—like the freedom to dress like hobos riding a
freight train, or wearing next to no clothes at all. They
demand that women be accepted by the armed forces,
even for combat (I've got enough combats to worry about,
thank you, without that!). I hear them demanding freedom *not* to wear bras. That's a *cause?*

When I ponder the platforms of some of these radical
feminists—the easy abortions; the demand of the right to
"do their thing" no matter who gets hurt as they do it; the
"liberated" women spouting about their "free life-
style"—I get a little sick and I ask myself, *Dear God—what
happens to the children of such free spirits?*

I see a form of child abuse in such lib.

Children are the gift—"an heritage of the Lord" (Psalms
127:3)—and they should be respected and treated as just
that. God honored women in making them the bearers of
children. These women, as I see them and listen to them,
appear to me to be casting aside a life-style ordained of
God for one that can only end up in a well of loneliness.
They talk of wanting their own careers. To me, no career
credits I have ever earned or received can measure up to
the credit of one "I love you, Mom," or, "I love you,
Grandma." A so-called free life, in my square opinion,
cannot compare to the thrill of the heart lift that comes

through the love of God, husband, and children.

Someone told me of a bumper sticker on the rear of a car which read HAVE YOU HUGGED A CHILD TODAY? I dig that sticker.

Our widespread breakup of the home that comes when the mother breaks away to get her "rights" is a very strong factor in child abuse. We are definitely off base when we practice it to this degree. We are cut away from our moral and spiritual moorings. No matriarchal society survives very long. It is unnatural, and not the way God meant it to be. Children need a father *and* a mother image in their development of good life patterns. When a boy is mother-dominated, with no strong father image, he is in danger of going badly off-balance. When a girl has no mother figure—unless the father is gentle as well as strong—she runs the risk of being off-balance sexually. The Lord knows that I am no authority on sexual deviation, but I have personally known such cases— particularly where the father is too busy or too weak—to give his children the necessary companionship.

Here is a case in point, relayed to me by a good friend, who tells of a family blessed(?) with a determined mother who does what she wants when she feels like doing it. If she wants to go off for a weekend of skiing, she goes, all by her lonesome. Sometimes she *does* leave a note on the breakfast table telling the husband and the kids that she hopes to be back by Monday. Her house looks like something shattered in the Battle of the Bulge; the windows haven't been washed or the curtains cleaned since they moved into the house ten years ago. She has three children. Two have "busted out" of college and the third is just plain hippie. The husband has just given up; he goes off to do *his* thing. Both let the devil take the hindmost, and he takes it.

The Bible has words of advice for this: ". . . the children ought not to lay up for the parents, but the parents for the children" (2 Corinthians 12:14). And, ". . . provoke not your children to wrath . . ." (Ephesians 6:4).

Maybe we should have laws to protect children from such neglect, but at the present time we have no such laws. There are plenty of laws defending *adult* rights, but none to guarantee such rights as good education, good homes, health care, affection, love, and security. Society can step in only after the abuse or neglect has become flagrant and reported to the authorities. That's wrong. Children are people, not things—and they have rights.

Career Pressure

Today, more than ever before, women are being pressured to leave home for careers and that has become a root cause of much neglect. I know that much of it is unconscious neglect, and I know that many women have talents and abilities for public service; and I know too that many mothers have to get out and work to support their children. But I also know that there are others who are not temperamentally suited for careers outside the home, but who are being made to feel inferior unless they strike out on their own. Such mothers tend to nurse a resentment against the children clinging to their apron strings. It is a real problem.

I have been a career woman since my teenage days, but for the past thirty years, since my commitment to God through Christ, I have *never* considered the career more important than the children beneath my roof. Roy and I

have raised seven children, and given them the very best
we could, and they have done well. But I confess to a
guilty feeling when I think of those long, long days when
we found it impossible to be at home and at work at the
same time. The very nature of show business made it
imperative that we move wherever and whenever the
"show" moved, but we still managed to keep our hands
on things at home. We turned down more than one
chance to perform in a highly profitable spot, because it
meant leaving the kids behind at home for too long a
time.

Now that the youngsters are grown and have families of
their own, we no longer have the problem—but the relent-
less pace of life "on the road" goes on. Right now, Roy
and I are flying to Norfolk, Virginia, where we will be the
guests of the "700 Club." I am scheduled to sing at the
New Creation Center at the Scope Auditorium also in
Norfolk; following that engagement, Roy will take off for
Philadelphia to accept a Liberty Bell award from the USO,
in recognition of our services to the men in the armed
forces at home and overseas. After that, he will be interviewed on the "Mike Douglas Show." I will fly from Norfolk to Chicago to be interviewed on the "Chicago A.M.
Show." Then, at last!—we will arrive separately at our
home in Apple Valley, just one hour apart. As Roy says,
"Dale goes one way and I go another, and we meet at the
pass."

Yes, we live in a bustling, on-the-move world. These
are fast and frantic days. I often feel as though I were on a
roller coaster and as I flit from place to place, I sense that
the world around me is on a roller coaster too, hurtling
along on a collision course. It makes me feel like shouting

to those around me, "Let's get off this roller coaster and get busy at our Father's business."

. . . And Sex

Sex abuse is so ugly and obnoxious that I wish I could just skip over it and forget it. But it is one form of child abuse that we cannot ignore, for the simple reason that, as Ron Horswell writes, "Reported cases of sexually abused children outnumber cases of physical abuse. Most child molesters are, surprisingly enough, not playground lurkers but rather the parents of the children they molest. The most typical situation is that of a natural father (not a foster parent or stepfather) sexually abusing his children with the mother's complicity. It seems to be common in middle and upper income families, as well as among the poor. Says Jolly K. (Founder of Parents Anonymous) 'Sexual abuse is common—it's something around your neighborhood all the time.' "

We have mentioned the fact that there are more than three million runaways in the United States; probably half a million of these have suffered sexual abuse or exploitation. Ellen Weber, in *Ms* magazine for April, 1977, writes:

> One girl out of every four in the United States will be sexually abused in some way before she reaches the age of 18. Although it is widely assumed that her assailant will be a mysterious pervert, according to a 1967 survey conducted in New York City by the American Humane Association, only one quarter of all sexual molesta-

tions are committed by strangers. Only 2 percent take place in cars; only 5 percent in abandoned buildings. In a full 75 percent of the cases, the victim knows her assailant. In 34 percent, the molestation takes place in her own home . . . . This is true of 44 percent of the female population of Odyssey House—a residential drug treatment program with centers in seven states—and out of their 52 cases on record only two had ever been reported to the authorities . . . . The National Center on Child Abuse and Neglect estimates that there are at least 100,000 cases of sexual abuse each year, though it is the most unreported category of criminal activity. Other professionals . . . consider a quarter of a million cases a conservative estimate.

There are statistics enough to convince us that sexual abuse may occur many times more often than mere physical abuse. A sad corollary to this is the fact that such abuse is too often ignored even when it is known. While every state specifically requires the reporting of physical abuse, nearly half the states do not specifically mention *sexual abuse* in their mandatory reporting laws.

There are several reasons why these offenses are not reported. The victim herself, overcome with a sense of shame when she realizes what has happened to her, hesitates to talk about it to anyone. The parents often "cover up" on the whole sad business, in an effort to prevent a situation that would destroy the home. Many wives keep silent out of fear of their guilty husbands. Neither the mother nor the child wants the neighbors to know about it, or wants to "go public" in seeking help that might solve the problem, and so they create a "hush-hush!" atmosphere in the home.

But—why go on? This whole thing is so repulsive that I hate even to think about it. But think we must. These parents are *sick, sick, sick*—and often slick in hiding it.

You've got the picture.

. . . And TV

TV violence is one of the worst child abusers in our modern society.

On the "Merv Griffin Show" one night, a young gangster talked about his life in the world of crime. He had been guilty of nearly every crime in the book, from petty theft to murder. When Merv asked him if he watched crime shows on TV, and if he did, *why*, the hoodlum said sure, he watched TV, but he watched *only* "shoot-'em-up" stuff, because he could get a lot of good tips and ideas about "how to get away with it."

It makes us wonder about the effect of TV on the children of today—and, for that matter, on the whole family. I am all for *good* TV, and there is a great deal that is good about it. But the flood of violence that pours out of the tube into our living rooms—I shudder when it comes.

What has happened to the family of yesteryear that read the Bible in family devotions, went to church together, went on picnics and to the county fair together? We've thrown all that out of the window, while the devil has sneaked in through the door. We are depending on spoon feeding by the media, and too much of the food we get is anything but good for our moral and spiritual condition. TV, and not the Lord God, is becoming our "family shepherd."

Listen to this, sent to me by a concerned friend:

The TV Psalm

The TV set is my shepherd. My spiritual growth shall want.

It maketh me to sit down and do nothing for His name's sake, because it presenteth so many good shows that I must see.

It restoreth my knowledge of the things of the world and keepeth me from the study of God's Word.

It leadeth me in the paths of failing to attend the evening (and sometimes morning) worship services, and doing nothing in the Kingdom of God.

Yea, though I live to be a hundred, I shall keep on viewing TV as long as it will work, for it is my closest companion. The sounds of its pictures, they comfort me.

It presenteth entertainment before me, and keepeth me from doing important things with my family.

It filleth my head with ideas which are contrary to those set forth in the Word of God.

Surely, no good thing will come of my life, because TV causeth me to backslide, and I will be ashamed before Him at His coming.

AUTHOR UNKNOWN

This is too harsh an indictment of TV? Maybe so. I would be the first to admit that there are some very good programs on the tube—ones that are wholesome and entertaining and instructive, such as "The Waltons," "The Little House on the Prairie," "Sesame Street," "Grizzly Adams," and religious broadcasts that should be more popularly watched than they are now. But when TV becomes a baby-sitter or a child-sitter with no monitoring on the parents' part, the children are *abused*. They are abused by the gangster orgies and by the comedians who think they have to be dirty to be funny.

We can't put all the blame on the producers of this stuff, or on the advertisers either. We certainly don't have to watch such programs, if we are offended by them. The fault lies primarily with the parents, who can see to it that the child watches what is good for him to watch and is not abused by programs that are so often indecent, even for adults.

I plead guilty of failure to monitor our TV. There were many days when our children were at home, and I was working "from can to can't"—from dawn to dusk—riding Buttermilk in the canyons with Roy and Trigger. Our TV was not monitored because we were not there to monitor it, and there is no telling what those kids watched, or for how long. Sometimes I have wished that we had never owned a TV set and that our children might have been forced to be creative in their playtime, as I was, as a child.

Or you may be thinking, "It's ridiculous to talk of going back to the Good Old Days. This is *now!*" You're right. This *is* now—and now is the acceptable time to do an about-face in the TV department. Now we can do what we failed to do as parents, yesterday: We can *organize to protest*. The time is right for that, for I understand that the TV producers are worrying about the widespread objections that are spreading across the country, and that they are setting up future broadcasts with a minimum of violence. I hope that's true, and I hope they *mean* it. I hope that TV violence suffers a sudden death, for the sake of the next generation.

4

The Solution(s)

So—what do we do about child abuse and with the abuser?

For better or for worse, up to the present time, we have tried to solve the problem with our prisons, our family and juvenile courts, our welfare system, our social-service systems, and in some cases, the public schools. Roughly speaking, we have used two approaches: criminal and civil.

Criminal Approach

Suppose we look at the criminal approach first.

Certainly, the abuser *is* a criminal, and he deserves a criminal's punishment. We can understand the outrage of our society when it cries out for punishment of the offender. "Throw him in prison where he belongs; make him pay for it!" But that isn't much of a solution. For one thing, it is a cry for vengeance more than a cry for punishment or justice; and for another thing it doesn't offer any permanent solution. A Salvation Army prison worker has said, "I am suspicious of our whole prison system; it's all wrong to me. It settles nothing, cures no one. It merely puts the prisoner out of sight for a while and then turns him loose worse than ever!" There is truth in that. We have been hopefully and wistfully saying that rehabilitation in prison is the answer—but what rehabilitation we have there is weak, to say the least. Many working in the field say it is a joke in most of our prisons, if it

75

exists at all. You can put a man behind bars for twenty years, and even if he serves all of it he comes out a broken, vengeance-minded man—and you can bet that he will repeat his crime and come back for another term.

"All right," say some well-intentioned folks, "if prison doesn't do it, then *kill* him, when he kills a child. He deserves it." I know how they feel, and I confess that more than once, when I have read of a child murder, I mutter to myself, *I could kill him!* Then when I cool off, I know I couldn't do that—I could never "pull the switch."

Our Victorville (California) *Daily Press* published a story of child abuse which seemed to me proof that the culprit involved deserved capital punishment. It told the story of the killing of a two-year-old boy by a man who had lived (unmarried) with the child's mother for about a month. When the man was arrested, the mother said that she wanted to marry him! She worked as a restaurant waitress, and she left the youngster with this monster to "baby-sit." The sitting ended in murder. The boy was pronounced dead on arrival at the hospital, death due to severe abdominal injuries caused by blows of a "blunt object." They found some forty bruises on the boy's body, including several small scars that could have been caused by burns.

This woman had experienced an unsuccessful marriage previously, before she went to live with this man "because she loved him"—in spite of the fact that she had seen him whip the child "maybe ten times." On one occasion, he had thrashed him severely with a belt, because the child had urinated on his shoe! And she *loves* that man? She is sick, and she needs psychiatric care.

And the man? May God forgive me, if I lack compassion

for him. I was so angry with that monster I thought capital punishment should be inflicted. At least that would put him out of the way and prevent him from doing it again to some other child. Then I read the words of Solomon: "A man of great wrath shall suffer punishment . . ." (Proverbs 19:19). I realized that I was guilty of wrath, and that wrath, punishment, and vengeance are God's concerns, not mine. "Vengeance is mine; I will repay, saith the Lord" (Romans 12:19).

Capital Punishment: Pros and Cons

Historically, in this country, we have inflicted the death penalty in good conscience—at least until the Supreme Court ruled against such penalty, when mandatory. But even when we were required by law to inflict it, I cannot imagine any juror enjoying the responsibility of condemning a man to death. I doubt that the judges involved relished imposing it, either. I believe that the rule of justice must stand for the protection of society, but whether we are justified in considering capital punishment as the *only* form of justice to be applied in all cases of murder— well, that bothers me. I know of instances in which the death penalty has been commuted to life imprisonment, and in many cases the prisoner has found forgiveness in Christ while serving that sentence; he has then worked with his fellow inmates to win them to Christ.

On a "700 Club" broadcast quite recently, I watched a filmed interview of an evangelist who worked with the condemned men on death row in one of our prisons. One inmate questioned by the evangelist told a story that burned itself into my heart. This man, surely guilty, had found Christ while he waited for his time to go to the chair, and knew that he was forgiven of God. He said then "Whatever God wills for me is all right; I am at peace." While he waited, he worked with the other doomed prisoners, trying to win them to the One who, by His atoning blood shed during *His* execution, gave to us cleansed hearts and the assurance of everlasting life. He was not clamoring for a reopening of his case; he was simply putting himself in the hands of God, admitting his guilt, and preparing himself for whatever might be his fate. He was utterly and completely sincere.

The Bible says, "For the wages of sin is death; but the gift of God is eternal life through Jesus Christ our Lord" (Romans 6:23). Even as Jesus healed to win souls to Himself, I believe He has made it possible for a man condemned to death to be reprieved for God's glory, and that that man can be used to win others to Christ. I believe that when a man like Chuck Colson (not a murderer) of the Watergate affair is given his freedom, that the Lord knows Chuck Colson's heart and is trusting him to do His bidding.

I believe that there are other punishments and consequences suffered by the murderer. Sin sets up a chain reaction. I know from personal experience that it produces a havoc that affects not only the sinner but innocent parties as well. Even though God forgives the sinner and the sinner feels the assurance of that forgiveness (that He "will remember your sins no more against you" [*see* Jeremiah 31:34; Hebrews 8:12; 10:17])—it is still hard for the sinner to forget. Sometimes I wonder, when a sinner on death row has his sentence commuted to life imprisonment, whether the sentence of living remembrance is easier to bear than quick death.

Let me leave it this way. I abhor killing, and in many cases it would be difficult—if not impossible—for me to impose the death sentence. But when it involves rape, torture, or the deliberate killing of a child, I believe I would be forced, in the name of justice and the admonition of Jesus about offending one of his little ones, to vote for the death penalty. And that would hurt me terribly.

You may be saying, "But that condemned person is the child of some grieving mother; how would you like to be in her place?" I wouldn't like to be in her place. Neither would I like to be in the place of the grieving mother of the victim, or in the place of some potential mother whose child might be murdered.

God of Justice

We Christians forget too much that God is a God of justice as well as a God of love and grace. Let me illustrate that with a look at my own experience. God has been making sure that, for the past twenty-nine years, I have been careful never to repeat some of the sinful things I did while I was running from His mastery for a quarter of a century. He has led me to pass through some very deep waters and to toil up some very tall mountains, in order to keep close to Him.

He did not simply say to me, "Dale, I forgive you; go your merry way." He said, "Follow Me; take up your cross and follow Me." The cross, for me, means to lift Christ high in my life, as well as to declare my faith orally; to walk the valleys He allows; to climb with His strength and grace the steep places I must climb; to be conformed, bit by bit, test by test, into His image. He cleansed my wounds but I still bear the scars. This is hard saying, but it is true.

When I hear about someone whose life is enmeshed in sinful difficulty, my scars *ache,* and I suffer for that person. People ask me, "Dale, why are you so uncomfortably honest about yourself?" Do you really want to know? I am that way because, *now,* my life is hidden with Christ in God, and I must of necessity be objective about my days of philandering and running from Christ.

Whenever I read about the sorry state of those messed-up lives, I can only say, "There, but for the grace of God, go I." I can never undo the consequences of my accumulative sins, but in God's strength I can refrain from repeating them and, like the woman at the well, I can be honest in telling others what God has done for me—and is doing—in my life.

Courts and Law

Then there are the courts and the law. By *courts,* we mean family, domestic, and juvenile courts, where child-abuse cases are heard. By *laws* we mean the protective laws—local, state, and national—which are supposed to protect the child and punish the guilty abusers.

It is estimated that there are some twenty-seven thousand juvenile or family courts in the United States, and according to many professionals in the field, most of them have a very, very low rating. Their feeling is that the courts cannot and do not do much to solve the problem. They do not believe that anyone learns to love in a courtroom or a prison. Dragging the parents into court may—if the child dares to tell the truth—produce nothing more than more abuse.

Add to this the fact that most family and juvenile courts are hopelessly overloaded and understaffed, with almost countless cases waiting to be heard. It often takes months before the case *can* be heard; then it can be delayed when the judge asks for further investigation or, due to the pressure of other cases already on his calendar, just postpones the hearing to a future date. Back in 1974, for instance, the Cook County (Chicago) Illinois Neglect Court had only one courtroom in which to try its cases, and in that courtroom there was often a case load of seventy to eighty cases *a day*. One prosecutor said that he was lucky if he could spend an hour preparing each case.

And what can the poor judge do? He can punish the parents with prison sentences, or he can put them on probation, promising that he will "throw the book at them" if they ever appear in his court again. Or he can send the child back home under supervision of court officers or social workers and watch what happens. Or he can take the child away from them and place him in a foster home or some other local institution. Most judges hate to do that. There is bound to be criticism when they are as drastic as this.

Naomi Feigelson Chase, in her book *A Child Is Being Beaten,* sums it up:

> What can we do about the courts? If they have lost their function of placing children, if they have never been successful in rehabilitating them, if they have such meager resources that their existence insures only that families brought before it undergo a bureaucratic, unsympathetic, often destructive experience with the law, what is the point in maintaining them?
>
> The time for reform and redefinition in the

family courts is long overdue. It is generally
agreed that the courts are a revolving door, that
they do not have the resources to help, that in
putting children through the court process, they
lose whatever little respect for law and order they
might have originally had . . . .

There are laws—good laws—behind the courts, which
are of vital importance. Every state in the Union has them;
all fifty states now have laws requiring the doctors to report to the proper authorities suspected cases of child
abuse or neglect. Those who knowingly fail to report such
cases can be fined fifty dollars or jailed up to ninety days.
On the whole those laws work well, in spite of the doctors
who hesitate to "inform" on parents who have been their
longtime patients.

Under criminal law, the abusive parent can be tried
and, if found guilty, sentenced on charges of assault and
battery (if the child recovers) or tried for manslaughter (if
the child dies). While the judge may understand that the
abusive parent needs counselling rather than confinement, he is still quite likely to hand down a prison-term
sentence.

Do Children Have Rights?

There is a problem within a problem, here—the problem of the "right" of the parent to bring up his child as he
pleases. We mentioned this briefly earlier in this book.
We mention it again, not so much to question the rights of
the parents, but to ask about the rights of the child.

The bitter truth is that the child has precious little protection and rights under the law. Mrs. Helen L. Butten-

weiser, a New York attorney, explains the child's predicament in these words:

> There are no statutes that specifically state what a child is entitled to. Adult rights, on the other hand, are stated very specifically and clearly. There should be statutes stating a child's legal rights—to a good home, education, health care, affection, love and security. As it stands, a child is really in limbo. In law and court actions, society can only step in after an allegation of abuse and neglect. The burden of proof is on society. I say that the burden of proof should be on the parents . . . .
>
> From *Somewhere a Child Is Crying*

We have a national Child Abuse and Neglect Reporting Law, first proposed in 1962. It is a well-intentioned law, but unfortunately we have a great many other-intentioned doctors who do not want to "get involved." In one New York county (a very respectable community) only 6 out of 891 cases of child abuse were referred to state agencies by doctors' offices. The doctors objected (and they may have something here) to spending a day and a half in family court waiting to testify for 5 minutes; others felt that it was wrong to keep 30 or 40 other patients waiting in their offices while they spent hours with an abused child. Medical schools, we are told, are searching for other methods of dealing with the problem in a better way. Let's hope . . . !

We also have a national Child Abuse Prevention and Treatment Act passed by Congress in 1974 to finance the U.S. Children's Bureau of the Office of Child Development. There are other bills being currently considered by Congressional committees.

But can national legislation solve the problem? Vice-President Mondale says no. "I probably devoted more time in the Senate to the special problems of children than to any other single issue. But the more government programs I looked at, the more convinced I became that there is no substitute for a healthy family. Nothing can give a child as much love, support, confidence, motivation, or sense of self-worth as a strong and loving family."

Effectiveness of Foster Homes

That leads us into another consideration: the civic foster home or institution. Some of us regard them a "necessary evil"—not good, but something we *must* have to provide shelter for the child in emergency situations. Others, who have had foster-home experience, tell us that the abused child is often worse off in the foster home than he is in his natural home. There may be some exaggeration in that statement. I have known, intimately, some good orphanages and privately maintained foster homes for abused or deserted children, but I am also sadly aware that there are just too many bad ones which may be doing more harm than good.

In a pamphlet "To Combat Child Abuse and Neglect," prepared by the Public Affairs Committee, Theodore Irwin writes out his estimate of our system of institutional care and protection:

> In the past (and in many communities, still) maltreatment cases were bucked around in fragmented, confusing fashion among various private and public agencies, the police, child care

institutions, public welfare departments, juvenile and family courts. Commonly, following a neighbor's report, a police officer would pick up a badly injured child, take him or her to a police station or juvenile court, file charges against the parents, and drop the child off at a shelter.

Without exploring alternatives, children were subjected to the devastating experience of being torn away from their families. There was, however, no sign that this traditional system prevented further tragedies or delinquency. Nor, under such intervention procedures, were the courts told when the parents were ready to resume care of their children. Judges have, understandably, been unwilling to risk returning a child to his home for fear he might be battered again, but too many children have remained in foster homes or institutions far too long.

Foster homes may remove a child from a hostile environment, but they have not provided a full answer to the problem. According to James T. Kent, a California pediatric psychologist, when a child is placed in foster care he doesn't belong to anybody. "The foster-care home is a caretaking arrangement—it cares for the children and protects them but doesn't love them as a parent would. Meanwhile, the system offers no therapy to parents . . . ."

It happens in all too many child-care institutions. I find it difficult to write about it, for in a way, Roy and I have established a foster home, not necessarily for abused but for neglected children. But, thanks to God who holds us in His arms of love, it has been a vastly different foster home. We have loved these children, and they have loved us. I am repelled at the thought that such love is definitely *not* to be found in so many other foster homes. I just can't imagine any "home" without love.

Institutional Abuses

This abuse exists, and we must reckon with it. Pick up your newspaper and you will be shocked to read of the number of custodial institutions that are being investigated, of children in solitary confinement for trifling misbehavior, underfed, poorly clothed, given little if any schooling or instruction in trades which would help them find employment later on. Many a "Correctional Center" or "School" is little better than a jail.

There is, by way of illustration, one school for mentally retarded children in New York. It was so bad that a lawsuit was filed by the parents of the children in the school. A legislative investigation revealed that the children were found dressed in filthy clothing and dying at the rate of two or three a week, often from choking on food. Some five thousand were living in buildings built to hold twenty-nine hundred. There were no training programs—no programs at all for the little prisoners. This may be the only one of its kind, but even one is too many.

The detention homes and jails are even worse. Investigative reporters have found children wearing handcuffs, with their feet tied to their hands, toilets overflowing, rooms reeking with urine or garbage, children confined in cells little better than dungeons, beaten with whips or belts. They also uncovered a mean group of institutional officials who were given a certain amount to pay for the food the children ate, who fed their charges food you wouldn't give to a stray dog—and put the money they saved in their own pockets.

Had enough? So have I. And wouldn't you think it is about time we did something about it, in the name of One who took the children in His arms and blessed them?

To put it in a nutshell, it is evident that the courts and the prisons are a total loss in their so-called solutions to child abuse. The social workers involved will admit that it is too much for them; they are not staffed or equipped to handle a problem of such proportions. Our welfare system is failing; many within that system have no training in this field. Our schools accomplish next to nothing; it may be too much for us to expect the schools to do it, for they are not organized for such a purpose. So what? Where do we turn; where do we go from here? Do we just give up and try to live with it, or is there something we can do?

Finding the Facts

We can do a lot, if we want to. We can stop passing the buck to the courts and the foster homes and the schools. We can stop being merely antiparent, offering punishment and little else for the erring father and/or mother. We can remind ourselves that an ounce of prevention is worth a pound of cure. We can make the effort to find out *why* the parents abuse the child, and we can sit down with them to discuss the behind-the-scenes problems that drive them to distraction.

What we have to do first is to ask ourselves the question: "What really *produces* this problem?"

Once that idea got firmly rooted in my head, I made up my mind to stop just being mad about it. I wanted to find out—from people who knew a lot more about it than I did—what was waiting to be done and what was actually *being* done. I picked up my phone and called two institutions in Los Angeles—ones that I knew were working on the problem—and told them I wanted to find out what it was all about. They said, "Fine. Come on."

One of these was the famous Childrens Hospital in Los Angeles; the other was the UCLA Medical Center.

Childrens Hospital

So I started out one beautiful morning for Childrens Hospital. The beauty was blurred a bit by an experience in the restaurant across the street from the hospital, where I had breakfast. When I went up to pay my check, the lady cashier recognized me and said she had read some of my books—for which I am always grateful! Then she asked me if there was some member of my family in the hospital. When I told her I was doing research for a book on child abuse, she shook her head sadly and said, "Well, you ought to see some of the abuse I see right here in this restaurant." I couldn't imagine such a thing happening in such a place.

She told this incident:

"Just the other day a young mother came in here, literally dragging a little boy across the floor. The child looked pale and almost unconscious; the mother looked fairly intelligent, but she seemed half out of her mind. She kicked the boy and yelled at him to get up and walk. The girl at the check stand said to her, 'That child is sick; you should be taking him to the hospital.' No, the mother said, he wasn't sick at all; he was just lazy. When she saw that this excuse wasn't getting through to the check girl, she explained that 'he fell on a rock . . . .' But she guessed maybe she *should* take him to the hospital . . . ."

I was still thinking of this child as I sat down to talk with Heather Halperin, who is a clinical social worker in the Family Development Program at the hospital. (Notice the emphasis on the word *family* in this title. It's important, as we shall see.) I asked Heather how she would proceed with the mother in the restaurant, if and when she came to the hospital.

"Well," said Heather, "it's a complicated process. The first thing I have to do is to report the case to the law-enforcement authorities in the district where the family lives. That isn't easy, and I do my best to convince the parent or parents that it is just routine—something I *have* to do, but I want them to understand that I really care, and want to help them rather than condemn them.

"From this point on, the family sees approximately four to six doctors, nurses, and social workers, who are constantly asking questions—perhaps the *same* questions. Eventually, it reaches the court, if the case is bad enough to merit court attention. From the time they are admitted to the hospital to the end of the court proceedings, there are five separate social workers intervening in their lives. That tends to complicate matters, and sometimes rouses resentment. But, you see, we *have* to talk extensively with the families, in order to know exactly what is going on. And we have to talk with the neighbors, too, to get the whole picture. It is a grim performance, from beginning to end, considering the number of cases in which we have to go through this routine.

"From January first to December thirty-first, 1977, we received one hundred two children who showed injuries consistent with possible physical abuse. Five of them died on the day of admittance. There wasn't much we could do about them. It was too late. If we had had a chance to deal with the *families* before the abuse began, we might have been able to save the lives of all five of those young children.

"A few of these babies and children come from affluent, quite respectable families in this city, but most of the families are *not* affluent or well educated. Only one family out of five is college-educated. In this one family we found a religious background and attitude—but we also found a determination to bring their children to a 'perfection' which the children were unable to attain. The parents were disappointed and deeply dissatisfied with the children's performance; it became an unhappy home, not at all like the 'model' homes we are supposed to find among the affluent middle or upper class. I've known many homes like it—homes in which the needs of the parents get all mixed up with the needs of the children, a situation against which they respond in bitterness. They tend either to neglect the needs of the child or to resort to violence on the child because they fail to understand his needs—or his *rights*."

(Think that one through! How often have you insisted that a child do so and so "just because I say so!" without giving the child a chance to explain his need?)

Doctor James Apthorp, pediatrician and the hospital Trauma Consultant, put in a word here: "A truly realistic and meaningful family-life instruction in the public schools would be a very helpful deterrent to child abuse . . . This does not simply mean sex education, but all the facts of family life."

This idea of bringing the whole *family* into a discussion of the problem underlies the program they have at Childrens Hospital.

Ms. Halperin told me that of the five dead babies (mentioned above), all were three years of age or under. She also said that the parents of these children mourned their deaths and suffered tremendous guilt. Almost all of them loved their children but were unable to control their frustrations. It was possible for these parents to be rehabilitated, for they had found at Childrens Hospital people who cared and who wanted to help. (The hospital *cares*, certainly, but it does not condone any harsh or unreasonable corporal punishment.)

When I asked Heather whether it might not be better to take the child away from abusive parents who inflicted "cruel and unusual punishment," she was careful with her answer. Temporary foster care, she said, was once the *only* solution. But today we know that while the temporary home provides *physical* safety for the child, the *emotional* damage of being shifted around from one home to another and feeling that you never belong anywhere is often destructive to the child's emotional balance. (Remember Oswald, Ruby, and Manson?) This is not to imply that foster homes are not valuable in many cases. The Family Development Program at the hospital does approve of it in certain situations and for such reasons as these:

1. Where one of the parents is severely emotionally disturbed.
2. Substance abuse, such as drugs, alcohol, etc., is involved.
3. Refusal of parents to accept treatment.
4. Where there is an unstable environment which can be treated during the temporary placement of the child.

In the end, the question of whether or not the child should be taken from the parents is up to the judge. So is the decision as to when he shall be returned to them, or given permanent foster care, or be adopted by other "parents." Termination of parental care is becoming more and more rare, but provision must be made for it, when it is necessary.

I left Heather with a very deep respect for her ability on this most difficult job, and for her contribution to the whole problem of child abuse. She had the courage to put her finger on what she felt was wrong with so much of our so-called treatment. She had genuine, refreshing love for both the child and the hurting parents. She said at the end of our visit, "I have been working here at Childrens Hospital for five years, and I have seen at least eight hundred cases of child neglect or direct physical abuse. There are times when I really get mad, times when a case 'gets to me.' But by and large, when I pull back and look at parents *as people,* what I see is *hurting parents.* They are hurting on another level than their children, but they hurt . . . ."

This sympathy with both child and parent may be the secret of her success in working with both of them. She

doesn't go for the old idea that children should be seen
and not heard, or with the other idea that children should
be taught respect for their parents with whippings and
beatings. What she is after is a realization on the part of
both child and parent that they should be open and understanding and truthful with each other.

As I left the hospital, she gave me a copy of a great
cartoon by Jules Feiffer which I want to share with you. It
contains words that might have been written by a little
girl for other little girls:

I used to believe that I was a good girl
Until I lost my doll—and found it wasn't lost; my big
   sister stole it.
And my mother told me she was taking me to the zoo—
Only it wasn't the zoo; it was school.
And my father told me he was taking me to the circus—
Only it wasn't the circus; it was the dentist.
So that's how I found out I wasn't good:
Because if I was good, why should all these good people
   want to punish me?

© 1976 by Jules Feiffer

Does that say something about mutual understanding
to you? It sure does to me.

UCLA

The University of California in Los Angeles (you probably know it as UCLA) started one of the most efficient
and comprehensive child abuse treatment centers in this
country. Known as the UCLA Child Trauma Intervention
Project, it was housed in a huge medical complex, at the

Neuro-Psychiatric Institute, The UCLA Medical Center. This facility is so huge that I wandered around in it for forty-five minutes before I found the office of Dr. Morris J. Paulson (Professor of Medical Psychology) and heard from him the story of a project that just would not give up.

This Child Trauma Project first began in 1968, staffed by psychologists, psychiatrists, nurses, and social service workers. From 1968 to 1974 it provided treatment to individuals and families needing help in parenting their children. Their clients included a wide variety of parents, from the mother who feared she might abuse her child to those who had already beaten or killed a child. Many parents came willingly, realizing that they needed help, while some were referred to the Project by the courts. The more defensive offered all sorts of excuses, or just plain lied about what had happened, or was about to happen to their children.

The explanations they offered would be almost comical were they not so tragic; for instance—"the child had fallen down a flight of stairs, he fell from his potty chair, he wet his pants, he cried so much, he had temper tantrums, he was forever crying at feeding time, he drank from his brother's bottle," and on and on. The UCLA program provided treatment for 115 mothers and fathers from 1968 to 1974. Only 10 or 15 percent of identified cases of child abuse reached the courts, these being the more severe cases. (We must remember that besides the great majority of cases that are caused by overwhelming isolation and emotional frustration, there is a small hard-core group of adults who are tragically cruel and brutal toward their children.) Many children who came to the UCLA Project were so abused that the courts had already taken custody of them. The courts would then place the parents under the control of the Department of Public Social Services for concomitant supervision and/or collaborative treatment.

Doctor Paulson had additional aspirations and dreams which were fulfilled by his being awarded a large federal grant from Maternal and Child Health, Department of Health, Education and Welfare—a long step forward. He subsequently developed five treatment centers in Los Angeles County, knowing there was a desperate need for immediate help, in areas close to where the parents lived. These court-referred parents met weekly in their home community, using churches, schools, and other neutral meeting places. (That was done to remove concern for "what the neighbors might think" if they were held in a psychiatric center.)

The parents came in with varied, illogical excuses—but instead of becoming angry and berating them, Dr. Paulson and his staff very wisely "turned the other cheek," listening to their explanations and excuses; calmed them down and began to talk with them in a low-keyed tone of voice. Doctor Paulson recognizes that "parents cannot, and many times will not admit that they are abusing parents. They need to shift the blame on to 'society.' " Realizing this self-protective need, further confrontation was unnecessary. The parents could then proceed from a position of acceptance to exploring other areas of family conflict.

This four-year federally funded program has contributed significantly to the better understanding of "at risk" parents. In those four years Dr. Paulson and his staff opened many new doors. They provided treatment for an additional 100 families, including 125 abused children. In this group were 12 families in which the "target child" either died or in which there had been the earlier death of a sibling (where, however, these cases had never been identified as child abuse). In other words, approximately 12 percent of these parents were directly responsible for a child's death.

Factors to Be Recognized

Based on his ten years of research, Dr. Paulson has set down five factors which must be recognized if we are to understand the causes of child abuse. They are:

1. What is the nature of the abusive parent's own childhood? Had he or she been abused as children? Is there the possibility of an abusive family heritage?
2. What is the quality of the present family relationship? Family harmony is vital. The parents must be able to share, communicate feelings, and be an emotional support to each other. Is there any religious faith in the home to support the parents when they are in stress? In the case of the single parent, there is no support person. Therefore faith in God is even more vital. If there is no other person to turn to, then the child becomes a scapegoat for the parent's frustration.
3. What are the individual personality characteristics of the parents? If the parent is withdrawn, uncommunicative, explosive, this spells danger to the child.
4. What are the individual characteristics of the target child itself? If one or both parents have pre-

conceived goals or expectations beyond the child's ability, then the child becomes increasingly at risk.

5. What reality factors triggered the abusive incident at that particular moment?

Doctor Paulson explores carefully these five factors in every case of child abuse in order to better understand why the child was abused. With this knowledge he can then plan for effective treatment. Nothing is more important than immediate intervention.

At the present time Dr. Paulson and his staff are busy with two new projects. One is the setting up of a clinic for sexually abused children, where they can receive specialized treatment. He also includes the parents in this project. In the other project he is seeking funds for a new program of Primary Prevention of Child Abuse. (Secondary intervention, he explains, is providing treatment *after* the abuse occurs; primary prevention is recognition of and treatment for high-risk families *before* the abuse takes place.) He wants especially to study child-rearing attitudes in prenatal mothers, in order to provide a positive family environment—one that is emotionally and physically nurturing. Doctor Paulson would take those parents who are aware of a "blessed event" about to happen and have them participate for the duration of the pregnancy, and perhaps longer in a preparation-for-parenting program. They would be given a number of personality and attitude evaluations. The staff would make observations of postpartum mother-child interaction immediately after delivery, as well as observe the same reaction during the hospital stay. The staff then plan to follow mother and child for three years with medical and psychological evaluations every six months. Over this three-year period Dr. Paulson hopes to be able to correlate the development of emotional and physical milestones with prenatal attitudes of the parents regarding child-rearing. He hopes ultimately to find clues that would identify which parents are "high risk" prior to birth.

What does he mean by "high risk"? Dr. Paulson illustrated this with the following example: Suppose Mary and her husband are told by their doctor that she is pregnant. Mary cries, saying, "We are not ready for a baby." The minute she says that, the doctor should know that she is in conflict about the pregnancy. Both parents should have professional help to explore why the family is not ready for the baby, and what can be done to help the parents to resolve these areas of anxiety and fear before the birth of the baby. Doctor Paulson recommends that classes be provided to help couples in preparing for parenthood, classes in which each can discuss his/her mixed feelings about being parents and learn, in addition, basic facts of child growth and development. When the baby then arrives, both mother and father will hopefully be ready to accept their parenting responsibilities. Such understanding of what it means to be a parent can prevent much child abuse.

Doctor Paulson told me of the case of a young mother married to a much older man (she was only in her late teens), and living three thousand miles away from any help from her family. Their baby was born healthy, but did have the perfectly normal habit of throwing up after feeding. Unaware that this was not unusual, and not knowing how to stop it, she felt herself a failure, and far from being a good mother. When the child continued to throw up, she began hitting him, out of sheer frustration. A pediatrician identified the bruises for what they were and referred the family to Dr. Paulson's program. When the staff reassured her that the baby's throwing-up was perfectly normal, she broke down, banged her fist on the table and cried, "Why didn't someone *tell* me?"

The point of this story is simply this: if the pediatrician had been able to tell her *before* she became so frustrated that there was nothing to worry about when baby "spit back" his meals, there would have been no beatings, no abuse. The mother, at that point, would have had the knowledge that would have helped her be a good mother. But, nobody told her . . . .

The family remained in Dr. Paulson's program for over two years. Her husband, who had given her insufficient emotional support after the birth of the baby, was also brought into the program. Two good parents then began to understand each other's needs and to grow closer emotionally.

National and Local Programs

One can go across this country from coast to coast and find many other groups and local organizations working on such new and enlightened approaches to the problem. On the national level, we have the Child Welfare League of America and the old and honored American Humane Society. We have more and more money being supplied through national and state legislation. There is the National Center on Child Abuse and Neglect, in the U.S. Children's Bureau of the Office of Child Development, in Washington, D.C.

In Nashville, Tennessee there is a Comprehensive Emergency Protective Services to Neglected Children, a federal project. There is also an Abuse Team working out of Vanderbilt Hospital, which diagnoses a battered child and recommends treatment. Buffalo has used a federal grant in its work among immigrant and other disadvantaged families. Denver (a trailblazer in the movement) has a startlingly effective Families Anonymous, and the University of Colorado Medical Center has a Battered Child Consultation Team. Boston organized the Trauma X Group, which has attracted national attention. SCAN (Suspected Child Abuse and Neglect) has been busy in Little Rock, Arkansas, where it was organized as a private, nonprofit group offering emergency and supportive therapy for abusing parents. And we all know what is going on in Los Angeles. These are typical of the new concern and the new approach.

Parents Anonymous

Living as I do in the Los Angeles area, I have been fascinated and inspired by the work of a group which should be awarded a Congressional Medal of Honor, in this fight. This is Parents Anonymous, better known as just "P.A."

P.A. got its start in 1970 with the efforts of a California mother of two children (abused children) and a deeply concerned psychiatric social worker, Leonard Lieber. The mother is known only as Jolly K. and she wants it to stay that way. Jolly K., as a child, had an abuse record that would frighten a hardboiled policeman. She knew what it meant to be abused and neglected! She was in and out of 100 foster homes and 32 other institutions; she never got beyond the fifth grade in school; she was raped when she was 11; she lived as a prostitute; had two marriages that blew up almost before the ink was dry on the wedding licenses—and finally made a good marriage, the third time around.

She had two little daughters, one of whom she called "the slut" and treated her accordingly. "My mother," she says, "always said I was a slut, and —— if I didn't believe her." Poor Jolly K. came to believe that she *was* a slut, and she took out her resentment on the girl, who nearly died under the treatment.

Jolly had no friends in those days; she had no place to go for help, even though she *wanted* help—badly. She describes what it is like for child abusers who have a sense of guilt: "Child abusers are going through hell. Sometimes they think they are going crazy. I can talk about it now; I live in bits and pieces of those feelings, but now I'm not in hell."

Leonard Lieber understood it; he listened to her cursing the lack of any place to turn to for help. He kept his temper and he asked her what she thought might be done about it. Lieber saw in this woman something more than a frustrated mother. His heart must have pumped faster when he heard her suggest that she was thinking of starting a therapy group made up of mothers who were living in hell. He didn't just say, "Good idea!" He put Jolly in touch with someone else whom he was seeing in therapy. The three met; it went well, and that was the beginning, as new group members began attending the get-togethers each week.

They called it Mothers Anonymous at first in Los Angeles. They started out on the basic idea that these mothers could help themselves and help others at the same time by sitting down together and "blowing off steam" and sharing their woes and their hopes. Then they set up a "hot-line" telephone system in which the mothers could dial in for help at any hour of the day or night. Yes—it was like Alcoholics Anonymous; their whole procedure resembled A.A. They arranged for mothers to send their children to each other, when the strain became unbearable.

It worked. Today they call it Parents Anonymous and it has some eight hundred chapters across the nation and a membership estimated at eight thousand—90 percent of whom were themselves, at one time, abused children. They had no money (later, they got a federal grant, which we hope will be renewed), but they had a lot of faith in what they were doing and they had at last a place where they could go to let it out before they took it out on their sons and daughters.

In the Parents Anonymous Manual, we read of how those attending the meetings should be approached by the chapter leader, who is a parent member in the group. A sponsor (assisting professional) can be a physician, or a psychiatrist, or a social worker, or a lawyer. The leader starts it going with something like this:

> You are entitled to your anger, to your rage. Everyone has these emotions. Everyone! The only difference between you and that sweet little mother across the street . . . is that you are not quite able to handle the actions of your anger. And that's just what Parents Anonymous is all about—to handle your anger and many other negative feelings . . . .

Parents Anonymous was *not* begun by a group of Ph.D.'s, or psychiatrists, or social workers who had theories, educated guesses and evaluations in mind; it was begun by ordinary parents from all walks of life (rich and poor, blue-blooded and mongrel) who were ready to admit that they had a problem in dealing with their children, and who felt that if they shared their emotions and their experiences they could help each other to overcome them . . . .

P.A. is *not* a "show and tell" program. If you want to tell your group what you did to your kids just to get it off your chest, that's fine, but you don't *have* to do that—ever. We are not here just to swap child-abuse stories, we want to get at the solution of how to stop our abusive tendencies and abusive behavior.

Just knowing that you are actually "taught" to be a child abuser aids greatly in overcoming your fears and tension. As an adult, you do not do everything your parents taught you to do . . . . and there's no reason why you must abuse your own children either. Understanding yourself and why you abuse children is more than half the battle . . . .

We encourage members to phone other members, especially if a member is at a panic-point of stress. There will undoubtedly be times when a member will need you, in person and in that member's home, to avoid abusing a child. They have to phone someone for help, someone who not only can get over to their place right away, but who *understands* what they are going through—they can't very well phone the fuzz [police]. There will be times when you yourself will need a member, and knowing that there is someone who really cares about *you* and *your* problems might make all the difference between an unpleasant memory . . . and a manslaughter charge. It's only fair to give other members what you expect them to do for you.

                    Reprinted by permission
                    of Parents Anonymous, Inc.

With this as a starter, they go to work—and their work is something to see and watch and cheer. I cheer for it, loud and clear. I buy it hook, bait, and sinker—especially when I am told that while there is the usual small percentage of backsliders among them, eight out of ten involved in the program have had their lives and their homes changed into what a poet once described as "something strangely new, and beautiful."

Heather Halperin, at Childrens Hospital, gave me a reprint of an article written for *Family Chatter,* published by Parents Anonymous in March of 1974. It sums up all I have been saying about P.A. in a letter which could have been written by a grateful child to his parents. It reads:

Dear Mom and Dad:
    You went to Parents Anonymous because you thought you weren't good parents. Maybe you feel bad when you yell at me or hit me. Well, I

don't like being hit, or yelled at, or told to stop bothering you, either, but I think you have forgotten to ask my opinion.

As I see it, you went to P.A. not because you were a bad parent but because you want to be a better one. I think that's great! And, even if you can't see the change, I can.

Every time you start to yell, hit or ignore my feelings and then stop, I learn self-control.

Every time you say, "I need to be alone." I learn about privacy and consideration of others. I may not quietly turn around and obey you, but I do learn the lessons.

Every time you recognize my fears and hurts without my telling you in words, I learn sensitivity.

Every time you see me as a person with feelings and treat me with dignity, I learn compassion.

Even when you do not yell or hit or ignore me, I learn a lesson. I learn that people have feelings, that they are not always kind and considerate. In that lesson, I learn reality.

So, Mommy and Daddy, I want you to know that in spite of the perverse little imp who lives within me and compels me to disobey you, even though I know the consequences, I thank you for trying to be a good parent. When you do something nice for me, I don't think about the fifty times you didn't, I remember the time you did.

If I have a special wish, it is, "Please, God, let

Mom and Dad learn to love themselves as I love them, so I can learn self-forgiveness."
Thank you. Peace.

YOUR CHILDREN

That is P.A., and it gets through to me, and it will get through to you, too, if you have eyes to see and ears to hear the children crying.

5

. . . And One Thing More

I have developed a very healthy respect and admiration for the opinions of the professional people I have met during the writing of this book—the doctors and the nurses, the social-work specialists, the psychologists, and the psychiatrists. I agree wholeheartedly with Dr. Fontana when he says, "I . . . believe that each community must take upon itself the responsibility for providing more and more and better day-care services, more and better training, and higher pay for child-care workers, more temporary shelter facilities, more lay therapists and parent aides and foster grandparents and homemakers. And I would certainly encourage the establishment and support of new chapters of Parents Anonymous." Amen, to that. Better words were never spoken.

Faith in God Is Vital

And I would add one thing more: the words of Dr. Paulson, as he described the factors that must be examined in eliminating child abuse:

> *"Family harmony" is vital.* Parents must be able to share, communicate feelings and be of emotional support to each other. Further, is there any religious faith in the home to support the parents in their stress? Even more, in the case of the single parent, there is no other support person: *therefore faith in God is vital.* If there is no one to

turn to, then the child becomes the scapegoat for
the parent's frustration.

That's it! I shall think of this as long as I live, think of it
every time I hear people say, "All we need when we are
sick is a doctor; he can do all that is necessary," without
appealing to God; or, at other times, those who say, "We
don't need doctors when we catch pneumonia; God can
do everything that needs to be done." I suppose you
could call that the old conflict between science and
religion—and it is as phony and ignorant as a three-dollar
bill. God gave us doctors, and their hands are His hands
probing to cure human pain. I say it again and again and
again, "We need *both* skilled professionals *and God; and
His love,* if we are ever to eliminate and prevent the neglect and abuse of children. With God's help, and with
the working relationship of parents and professionals,
child abuse can become a horror of the past."

The widespread breakup of the home is a major factor
in child abuse. Divorce has bombed too many homes out
of existence. Someone has said, "The three stages of modern family life are matrimony, acrimony, and alimony."
Bitter, but true—all too often.

More than two hundred years ago William Aikman
said: "Civilization varies with the family, and the family
with civilization. Its highest and most complex realization
is found where enlightened Christianity prevails; where
woman is exalted to her true and lofty place as equal with
the man; where husband and wife are one in honor, influence, and affection, and where children are a common
bond of care and love. This is the idea of the perfect family."

Correct! The Christian home is the Master's workshop.

The child needs both mother and father, not one or the other. Children need to be disciplined in love, to be protected from things that hurt. If we parents could only understand that the family is ordained of God and that split families are the work of the devil, how much better we would be!

In the home, and in our hearts, we should also understand this: that the ugly thing called *child abuse* is, after all, a *spiritual* problem. It is a problem of sin that must be wiped out in the practice of the presence and love of God as we saw it in Jesus Christ.

Love! Love! Love!

Love! Did you watch that TV telecast in which Pelé, the world's greatest soccer player, said good-bye to America? Pelé didn't ask that crowd of seventy-six thousand people to support his game financially and make it a popular, well-paying sport. He cried out to them, "Say it after me: 'Love! love! *love!*' " They shouted it in a facility dedicated to athletic competition, and it was the greatest thing that has yet happened in that stadium—or ever can happen. Pelé, as time wears on, may be forgotten as a great athlete, but his call to us to put love first will never be forgotten.

Without love we can do *nothing*.

Many times, you know, in our zeal to make our children into the sort of men or women we would like them to be, we fail—fail because (in love) we drive our children into confusion and emotional imbalance. We mean well, but we must learn to love wisely instead of just too much. Usually this is well intentioned, but when we misdirect our love and hopes for them, we push too hard and we

forget that God is responsible for their creation and that
He holds the blueprints of their lives in the hollow of His
hand. It really isn't a very effective love when we take it all
into our own human hands. I have been guilty of this, and
I admit now that I was wrong. But at the time I thought I
was doing what had to be done, and I was determined
that my children would not repeat my mistakes.

Love is a dynamic quality; we have to be careful how
we handle it—how we "pass it on."

Perhaps I can explain my thinking here by telling you
about Ruth Stapleton, a sister of our president and a
born-again Christian in her own right. She teaches
healing—the inner healing of the right kind of love.

Our local newspaper, the *Daily Press* in Victorville,
California, ran an article on her; it was headlined "President's Sister Tells of 'Wrong Love,' " and went on to say:

> . . . Ruth Stapleton, of Fayetteville, North
> Carolina, told 45,000 people gathered in a reli-
> gious conference in the Arrowhead Stadium in
> Kansas City how she drove her ten-year-old
> daughter into emotional problems with "the
> wrong kind of love . . . ."
>
> She gave her own personal account of her
> home life, which included "human mistakes"
> that she had made in trying to develop loving
> family relationships.
>
> After driving her daughter into emotional
> problems which required psychiatric treatment,
> said Mrs. Stapleton, an inner healing occurred.
> The healing, however, "didn't come from
> psychiatric therapy but from prayer," she said.

"The Lord bridged the gap between the love she needed and the love I gave . . . . The Lord can redeem every mistake we make with another human being." She said she learned that she did not "have to act like I'm perfect. Jesus Christ is the only example we can have. He is the one who is going to bring us into perfection.

"We've been hurt and we wrap ourselves in a cocoon, and we slowly die," she said, "but when we can communicate Christ's love, we can experience *inner healing*."

Now let's apply what Ruth Stapleton is saying to the problem we are facing.

The Cure for Child Abuse

I believe that the decisive cure for child abuse lies in bringing the abuser to the healing power of God through Christ—in their becoming new creatures in Christ—in being born again, and in experiencing His healing power. They will find that God can accomplish in their children what they have failed to accomplish.

When we consider the stench of moral decay in our country, the apostasy of the church, the apathy among lukewarm Christians about the appalling conditions of life today, we are compelled to pray that the Gospel of faith and love be preached quickly and constantly throughout God's world. We need a deep conviction of the truth that Jesus Christ *saves*—that He saves individuals, families, and nations—saves all who will come to Him. When He said, "Occupy till I come" (Luke 19:13), I believe that He meant that we should live for Him *every*

day of our lives, for His sake and for our sake, and for our
children's sake. When fathers and mothers recognize Him
as their spiritual head, I am certain that we will see a
turnaround in stabilizing marriage and family relation-
ships. And I think there will be a turnaround in our children, too—a turning back to respect for their parents (if
the parents be worthy of respect!) and homes blessed with
gratitude and love.

We can rationalize, computerize, philosophize—you
name it—but nothing will save us and our society but true
repentance for our individual and collective sins, seeking
Him with all our hearts, minds, and souls, and loving one
another as ourselves. To those who would reject God and
His Christ and say in their hearts that He is no more than
a man—that His miracles are myth and that man is
supreme—I reply that they insult God and that He will
hold them in derision.

My Bible tells me that "The Lord is in his holy temple,
the Lord's throne is in heaven: his eyes behold, his
eyelids try, the children of men" (Psalms 11:4). You say,
"What has this to do with child abuse?" I say, *"Everything!"*

When one is born again through complete submission
to Jesus Christ as Saviour and Lord, Master of every facet
of life, *then* the Holy Spirit begins to operate, *then* attitudes change and circumstances change; *then* we start to
"gentle down," and become more loving, more understanding of the problems of others. *Then* parents begin to
look at themselves as examples to their children. These
children of ours are not easily fooled; they are wiser than
we think, and if they see God is helping their parents to
be better parents, they will be more receptive to Christian

training. But they must first see it in action, *in us.*

Again, to put it in a nutshell, let me repeat this: I believe that child abuse can be stopped cold when parents seek intelligent clinical help *and* God's help. I believe it takes *both.*

I also believe Jesus Christ when He says to me, ". . . without me, ye can do nothing" (John 15:5).

Let me repeat it once more: The basic problem that we have in child abuse is a three-letter word—SIN—rebellion against God.

The Reality of Demons

A good friend of mine, with whom I was discussing a book on the exorcism of demons, said to me, "Oh, I don't think people have demons today; it's just mental problems." I disagree. While I am repulsed by some of the unnecessary horror in the movie entitled *The Exorcist,* I must confess that judging by the behavior of, let's say, the incorrigible child abusers, it seems to me that the demons are alive and well and still in business among us. I believe this because Jesus believed in demons and in sensible, spiritual exorcism of them, He was quite explicit about mental problems of the man of Gadara (Mark 5) who tore his clothes off, broke his chains, ranted and raved . . . . He commanded *demons* to come out of the man. Jesus, in that confrontation, asked the man, "What is thy name?" and the man answered, "My name is Legion, for we are many." Get it straight, it was the *demons* who were causing the mental problems, with their attendant violence. I believe this happens in many cases of child abuse: an evil spirit is in the abuser. He is filled not with the Holy Spirit of love, but with the very spirit of evil, and when that spirit is allowed to function—violence and destruction follow. Satan is very aptly called the Destroyer, and only the spirit of love, which we see in Jesus Christ, can in the end overcome him.

6

Help!

A Lesson to Remember

A wise old church school teacher with a class of high-school boys, some fifty years ago, found himself scheduled to teach a lesson on sin and punishment. He did an unusual and dramatic thing in teaching that lesson. He told his boys that the next Sunday they wouldn't meet at the church, but at his house, and from that house they were going to take a ride in his car. It looked like a lark—but it wasn't. He took the boys on a visit to the county jail, where they walked around with the prisoners and listened to them talk, and came out of it scared half to death. They just hadn't known what went on in a jail full of sinners.

Then he told them to write out what they saw, what they thought had put those prisoners in such a repulsive prison, and what they thought ought to be done about it. That one lesson went on for a month of Sundays, and at the end of it all, the boys agreed on two points: (1) the county jail was "no good for anybody"; and (2) *something* ought to be done about it.

Good! But they found they had a problem. Where should they start? And where could they look for help?

"Aye," as Mr. Shakespeare would say. "That is the question." Where can we turn, as concerned average citizens, for guidelines in an all-out effort to do something about this terrible sickness of our times?

I do not want to leave those who read this book with

just a feeling of helpless anger—which will fade, like all other anger—if they do no more than get temporarily indignant, so I am adding a few suggestions here that may help them get started.

Recognizing the Signs

First of all, they should be able to recognize the early signs of child abuse in the child himself, before reporting what they see and hear to the proper authorities. Doctor Fontana helps us here, with a list of factors or signs that indicate abuse in the victims:

1. The child seems unduly afraid of his parents.
2. The child is unusually fearful generally.
3. The child is kept confined, as in a crib or playpen (or cage), for overlong periods of time.
4. The child shows evidence of repeated skin or other injuries.
5. The child's injuries are inappropriately treated in terms of bandages and medication.
6. The child appears to be undernourished.
7. The child is given inappropriate food, drink or medicine.
8. The child is dressed inappropriately for weather conditions.
9. The child shows evidence of overall poor care.
10. The child cries often.
11. The child is described as "different" or "bad" by the parents.
12. The child does indeed seem "different" in physical or emotional makeup.
13. The child takes over the role of the parent and

tries to be protective or otherwise take care of the parent's need.

14. The child is notably destructive and aggressive.
15. The child is notably passive and withdrawn.
16. The parent or parents discourage social contact.
17. The parent seems to be very much alone and to have no one to call upon when the stresses of parenthood get to be overwhelming.
18. The parent is unable to open up and share problems with an interested listener, and appears to trust nobody.
19. The parent makes no attempt to explain the child's most obvious injuries or offers absurd, contradictory explanations.
20. The parent seems to be quite detached from the child's problems.
21. The parent reveals inappropriate awareness of the seriousness of the child's condition (that is, of the injury or neglect) and concentrates on complaining about irrelevant problems unrelated to the injured/neglected appearance of the child.
22. The parent blames a sibling or third party for the child's injury.
23. The parent shows lack of control, or fear of losing control.
24. The parent delays in taking the child in for medical care, either in case of injury or illness, or for routine checkups.
25. The parent appears to be misusing drugs or alcohol.
26. The parent ignores the child's crying or reacts with extreme impatience.

27. The parent has unrealistic expectations of the child: that it should be mature beyond its years; that it should "mother" the parent.

28. The parent indicates in the course of conversation that he/she was reared in a motherless, unloving atmosphere; that he or she was neglected or abused as a child; that he or she grew up under conditions of harsh discipline and feels that it is right to impose those same conditions on his or her own children.

29. The parent appears to be of borderline intelligence, psychotic, or psychopathic. (Most lay persons will find it difficult to make a judgment here. It might be better for the observer to note whether the parent exhibits the minimal intellectual equipment to bring up a child; whether the parent is generally rational or irrational in manner; whether the parent is cruel, sadistic, and lacking in remorse for hurtful action.)

From *Somewhere a Child Is Crying*

7

Types and Treatments

It is easy to generalize about child abuse, and to say that the abusers can be classified under just four headings: physical, verbal, emotional, and sexual. But it is a lot more complex than that. I followed this simpler formula in this book, but I must admit that there were some classifications that I could not cover in the space I had to tell my story in general terms.

I became conscious of this when I talked with Dr. James Kent, a Ph.D. in psychology and the principal investigator in child-abuse cases at the Family Development Research Project at Childrens Hospital in Los Angeles. He gave me the following "typologies" of child abuse, which he bases on the work of four researchers in the field, and which he uses in the treatment of families.

The four researchers listed the following categories of abusers, and their parental characteristics:

FIRST RESEARCHER

Hostile, aggressive parent. Continuous and uncontrolled anger stems from parent's internal conflicts. Parent has childhood history of severe emotional rejection and deprivation.

Rigid, compulsive parent. Parents defend their right to punish their children, whom they perceive responsible for the parent's trouble. Parents lack warmth and protectiveness toward their children and make excessive demands of them.

Passive, dependent parent. Parent is dependent, immature, and prone to depression. Within the family unit, the parent competes with the child for the love and attention of the spouse.

Physically disabled father. Fathers out of work, frustrated, and responsible for the care of the child while the mothers work. They suffer loss of status as well as loss of physical abilities.

SECOND RESEARCHER

Overflow abuse. Child abuse is rooted in an overflow of the parent's own frustration and irresponsibility. Abuse is repetitive, but not directed to any one child. The mother is most often the abuser and the father usually does not live in the home. Abuse is uncontrollable.

Disciplinary abuse. Parents are rigid, controlled, and unfeeling. They defend their right to discipline their child (usually an adolescent), for failing to comply with their expectations. Often they are upstanding citizens. Abuse is controllable.

Battered child. Severe abuse of infant is perpetrated by parent with high dependency needs, who sees the child as a burden or competitor who has to be destroyed. Often, only one child in the family is abused. Abuse is uncontrollable.

Misplaced abuse. Abuse is due to misplaced parental hostility which stems from marital conflict. The abuser is usually the father. The child abused is, generally, of illegitimate conception or birth, brain-damaged, or a pawn in marital conflict. Abuse is controllable.

Mental illness. Abuse is unpredictable, but ritualistic rather than impulsive. No particular psychiatric diagnosis is made. Abuse is uncontrollable.

THIRD RESEARCHER

Pervasively angry and abusive parent. Abuse is an impulsive and unfettered expression of general rage and hostility, which is part of the parent's childhood-determined personality. There is no pattern to the abuse. Most often the mother is the abuser and father does not live in the house. Abuse is uncontrollable.

Cold, compulsive disciplinarian parent. Abuse is reaction to the child's need for closeness and affection, and interest in body and sex. Parents have compulsively clean homes. They defend their right to punish their children. Abuse is controllable.

Depressive, passive-aggressive parent. Abuse represents anger and resentment at having to meet the needs of others, and at inability to meet the role expectations of a caretaker. Often only one child is abused, which is seen as a competitor or burden to the dependent parent. Abuse is uncontrollable.

Parent with identity/role-crisis. Abuse represents the father's displaced anger at loss of capability for previous role performance. The father stays with children while mother works. Abuse is controllable.

Impulsive (but generally adequate) parent with marital conflict. Abuse is the result of marital conflict displaced onto the child. It is often limited to one child who is a pawn in the conflict or is illegitimate, and so forth. The father usually abuses. Abuse is controllable.

Psychotic parent. Abuse is unpredictable; and ritualistic; it has idiosyncratic meaning related to the fantasies of the abuser. Abuse is uncontrollable.

FOURTH RESEARCHER

The inadequate personality. Same as second researcher's "Overflow abuse" with the added observation that neglect, as well as abuse, is characteristic of family.

Cold, compulsive disciplinarian. Same as second researcher's "Disciplinary abuse."

The passive-aggressive personality. Same as second researcher's "Battered child."

The displacement of aggression. Same as second researcher's "Misplaced abuse" with the exception that the abuser is usually the mother.

The psychotic personality. Same as second researcher's "Mental illness."

The sadistic personality. Parent has history of sadistic behavior and shows no anxiety or guilt for abuse. Often there are marital problems and alcoholism in family. Abuse is uncontrollable.

So there it is—in all its bewildering complexity. Really, while it all simmers down to four general reports, it contains much more than four types of abusers, each of which calls for different treatment. That word *uncontrollable* bothers me. It is a bit too pessimistic for those who think that there may be one simple answer to all of it—but there isn't. That's why we need the help of the doctors, social workers, and psychiatrists. It's like the problem of poverty; remember, Jesus said that the poor will be always with us (*see* Matthew 26:11).

But many of these so-called types have found answers and help in institutions like the Childrens Hospital, and in the practice of a love instituted of God and revealed in the love-sacrifice of His Son.

8

Agencies

Now that we are aware of the different types of child abusers, to whom or where may we, as good and concerned neighbors, go for help in our desire to understand and possibly stop or correct such abuse when we see it?

Emergency Calls

If it is a case of emergency, there is always your telephone! Use it. If it is a case involving violence, you need immediate help, and that means calling the police—but don't call the police unless it is absolutely necessary, or as a last resort.

If you have time, a call to your doctor or to your local church pastor might help. And you will find in your phone directory the names of other sources of help; they may be listed as a Child Protective Society, or Child Welfare Committee, or Social Service, and so forth. There is always your Board of Health, which could certainly refer you to the proper organization.

Every state in the Union has organized groups working on this problem and you can get information by correspondence.

National Organizations

On the national level, there is:

National Technical Information Service
5285 Port Royal Road
Springfield, Virginia 22161

It is far and away the finest source of information in the United States. It publishes a comprehensive and complete list and description of child abuse and neglect *programs* actively at work in every state, city, and county in the country. Disseminated under the auspices of the Department of Health, Education and Welfare, it is obtainable from the above address, for $11 (USA) or $13.50 to addresses outside the USA. (Prices are subject to change.) It is a tool of inestimable value.

The National Committee for Prevention of Child Abuse strives to increase public awareness and education about child abuse and its possible solutions; to provide a focal point for child and family advocacy; to identify resource centers, treatment centers, and agencies that can effectively deal with the complex issues of child abuse; to encourage the development of innovative programs directed toward the prevention of child abuse; and to bring together diverse professionals, lay citizens, and programs from around the country to develop one coordinated, integrated program. Address:

National Committee for Prevention of Child Abuse
Suite 510
111 East Wacker Drive
Chicago, Illinois 60601

Parents Anonymous, Inc.
2810 Artesia Boulevard
Redondo Beach, California 90278

This organization has been described in this book, as one of the highly effective organizations in the United States offering direct help. Find out whether there is a local chapter in your community, or in a city nearby, or write them at their California headquarters.

> The Child Welfare League of America
> 67 Irving Place
> New York City, New York 10003

This is a veteran organization working on a national scale. It is the national accrediting and standard-setting organization for public and voluntary child welfare agencies in the United States, offering definite programs of children's aid.

The Children's Division of the American Humane Association is a national federation of individuals and agencies working toward prevention; it specializes in alerting the public legislators of need for action, and conducts continuing research projects and surveys. Write them at:

> P.O. Box 1226
> Denver, Colorado 80201

Pamphlets dealing with child welfare, family life, and so forth, are available from:

> Public Affairs Committee, Inc.
> 391 Park Avenue South
> New York City, New York 10016

I think that if the abused children could speak to us, they might say something like this:

Listen to Us

If a child lives with criticism,
    She learns to condemn.
If a child lives with hostility,
    He learns to fight.
If a child lives with ridicule,
    She learns to be shy.
If a child lives with shame,
    He learns to feel guilty.
If a child lives with tolerance,
    She learns to be patient.
If a child lives with encouragement,
    He learns confidence.
If a child lives with praise,
    She learns to appreciate.
If a child lives with fairness,
    He learns justice.
If a child lives with security,
    She learns to have faith.
If a child lives with approval,
    He learns to like himself.
If a child lives with acceptance and friendship,
    She learns to find love in the world.

From *Children Learn What They Live*
(A poster distributed by Parents Anonymous)